Thoughts
of an
Average Joe

*A collection of humorous commentaries expressing
the concerns of Smalltown, New England's Joe Wright,
an ordinary, middle-aged man struggling to understand
and cope with life in the twenty-first century.*

Other Humor Books from Islandport Press

Not Too Awful Bad
by Leon Thompson

Headin' for the Rhubarb
and *Live Free and Eat Pie!*
by Rebecca Rule

John McDonald's Maine Trivia,
A Moose and a Lobster Walk Into a Bar,
and *down the road a piece*
by John McDonald

A Flatlander's Guide to Maine
by Mark Scott Ricketts

Finding Your Inner Moose
by Susan Poulin

Bert and I . . . The Book
by Marshall Dodge and Robert Bryan

Thoughts
of an
Average Joe

by Brian Daniels

ISLANDPORT PRESS

Islandport Press
P.O. Box 10
Yarmouth, Maine 04096
www.islandportpress.com
books@islandportpress.com

First Islandport Edition, April 2014

ISBN:978-1-939017-26-0
Library of Congress Card Number: 2013922644

Publisher: Dean L. Lunt
Book jacket design by Karen F. Hoots / Hoots Design
Book design by Michelle A. Lunt / Islandport Press
Cover photo courtesy of Dean L. Lunt

For
Mom and Dad

Acknowledgments

Thanks, Laurene, for being my "little woman" and best friend for almost forty years now. You are always there for me when I need encouragement, a reliable sounding board, or a reality check. I know it is—at times—not easy living with a smart aleck. Thanks for being a good sport and for letting me know when I'm being an idiot.

Dean Lunt, I appreciate your belief in this book. Thanks to you and your entire staff for the tireless dedication to making this project, like all Islandport Press projects, look good and read well. You've somehow figured out how to pay painstaking attention to detail and style, yet keep the editing process exciting and fun.

Thanks to John Cruickshank of the *Northfield News* and Glen Parker of the *White Mountain Journal* for sharing Average Joe's "Thoughts" with their readers for the past several years.

I'm blessed with family and friends who are not only supportive but are fascinating characters themselves. They've served as inspiration for the many, thinly disguised "Small-town" characters in this book. I know you know who you are, and I hope you know how much you mean to me.

Contents

A Few Words from the Author

When I started writing the newspaper column, "Thoughts of an Average Joe by Joe Wright," several years ago, I was often asked, "So Brian, why the *nom de plume?*" Since my fluency in French is limited, I assumed that folks were badgering me about my hairstyle. Once I realized they were inquiring about the pen name, I explained that, first of all, "Thoughts of an Average Brian" just doesn't have the same ring to it. More importantly, Joe's "Thoughts" occasionally differ from my own, and are often more entertaining.

This book contains the humorous ramblings of a middle-aged, thick-around-the-middle man who tends to lean a little right of middle-of-the-road. He hails from Smalltown, a quintessential northern New England hamlet, and struggles to understand and embrace the ways of the modern world.

Joe's commentaries voice his angst over dealing with life in the twenty-first century, as expressed in "I'm Not Ready for the Wireless World," or with eccentric family members whose stories are revealed in articles like "My Uncle Bing Liked to Fight." There is a long list of issues that annoy or confuse Joe, as he explains in the likes of "Poachers Ain't Hunters," "I'd Vote for an Honest Politician," and "So, What *Is* Victoria's Secret?" He, like most men, struggles to understand his "little woman," and others of her gender. Several articles, including "I'm Afraid of the Little Woman," and "Childbirth Can Be

Painful," address the frustrations of a man trying to get a fix on the inner workings of his wife, Winnie.

"Thoughts of an Average Joe by Joe Wright" has appeared for several years in publications throughout northern New England, allowing regular readers to become familiar with Joe, his family and friends, Dan's Market, Small-Mart, Blake's Esso Station, and the *Smalltown News*. As each essay was written as a stand-alone column when originally published in newspapers, some scenes and phrases appeared in more than one story. Consequently, to limit repetition, I've taken the liberty of changing the content of some chapters for inclusion in this book. A few redundancies are inherent in a compilation of this type, and remain.

In many ways, I wish I could be more like Joe Wright. I like the way he thinks. I hope you will too.

Introduction: Welcome to Smalltown

THEY SAY YOU ARE WHAT YOU EAT.

I don't think so. If that were true, I'd be some Hostess snack cake. I'd be a Ding Dong, or I'd act like a Twinkie or some cheap Ho Ho. Folks aren't what they eat; they are a product of their hometowns—the places where they grew up.

My name is Joe Wright. To know me is to know my town—Smalltown. It's the people, the schools, the churches, and the culture of this place that fostered the opinions, values, and attitudes that make me—for better or worse—the man I am today.

Smalltown is typical of the many little hamlets dispersed between the lakes and mountains of northern New England, and, still, unique unto itself. Let me take you on a tour of Smalltown. Most of this tour will describe life in my town as it was in 1962, when I was ten years old.

Growing up, I assumed every town had a big, two-story building with a giant replica of the familiar, green Bag Balm can jammed kitty-corner into its side as though it fell from the sky and crashed, like a meteor, into the wall of the factory. I knew Bag Balm was made in Smalltown, but had no idea it was made *only* here. I figured something so essential to the survival of the bovine, human, and even canine species of this planet must be produced in every village. I was certain Smalltown couldn't produce enough golden salve to treat all the chafed teats, cracked hands, chapped lips, and injured paws of the world.

I was wrong. Bag Balm is Smalltown's claim to fame and, to my way of thinking, something to brag about. I was proud to wear the uniform of the Smalltown Balmers. I wonder if Green Bay, Wisconsin, is honored to be the Toilet Paper Capital of the World. (Look it up.) Do opposing high schools play sports against the Green Bay Buttwipes? What does their mascot look like? If I hailed from Fort Payne, Alabama, I'm not sure I'd be excited about growing up in the Sock Capital of the World. That's not the kind of information that's likely to help a guy score on Ladies Night at the Bear Den Tavern.

The Miss Smalltown Diner is a place folks go for their minimum daily allowance of caffeine, Crisco, and gossip. It not only provides a steady stream of patients for the Northeast Cardiac Care and Vascular Surgery Center; it also feeds the town rumor mill, and serves as a research center for the *Smalltown News*.

Station Street is the main drag in downtown Smalltown. It is so named because, for many years, Smalltown had a train station at the east end of the street. As a kid, I liked walking on the wooden platform outside the station. It was like we had our own boardwalk, but without the Speedo-clad old men, corn dogs, cotton candy, and palm readers.

The Canadian Pacific Railroad brought a lot of workers to Smalltown from Quebec. They were Catholics, spoke French, worked hard, and played hard. My mother's father, my *pépère*, worked for the railroad, so we lived on Eastern Street, in one of the dozens of look-alike houses built by Canadian Pacific.

Mom and Dad had six of us Wright rug rats over the course of twenty-two years. Mom was Catholic; Dad was Persistent.

Nearly every home on Eastern Street was brimming with kids. There was never a shortage of playmates with names like Goyet, Laferriere, and St. Onge, for football in the fall or baseball in the spring. The French-Canadian Catholics of Eastern Street produced a steady stream of children, all raised on a diet of *tourtière* (meat pie), baked beans, and guilt.

Station Street is approximately a hundred yards of bustling commerce. This was especially true on double-stamp day at Dan's Market. Every Thursday, Mom, *Mémère*, and essentially every other woman in the greater Smalltown area would fight for a parking spot, wait in line to get into Dan's, play a two-hour game of shopping-cart demolition derby, and then stand in the checkout line for forty minutes. The reward? Twenty extra S&H Green Stamps to be pasted into little books which were collected for twelve months, at which time they could be redeemed for a pair of dinner plates that matched nothing else in the cupboard.

Station Street is the Madison Avenue of Smalltown—minus the traffic lights, fancy stores, bright lights, and glamour. There's a grocery store anchoring each end, two clothing stores (one for each gender), two restaurants—one that serves American fare (burgers, steak, and chicken) and the other which serves . . . well . . . the same stuff—and there's also a hardware store and two drugstores.

Smalltown IGA was owned by my father when I was a kid. Our store was one of those with crates of cherries, apples, peaches, and pears stacked outside during the three warm months. Folks like Nuckie Leonard, who wouldn't dream of stealing a piece of penny candy, would stand outside the store and eat 50 cents' worth of cherries—spitting the pits onto the sidewalk for me to sweep up later—while telling Alphonse Lebrecque about his recent hemorrhoidectomy.

There were no credit or debit cards back then, so Dad would let people run a tab. Of course, they ran a tab because they couldn't afford to pay cash for their essentials—you know, Schaefer beer, potato chips, and Lucky Strikes—and they never did. Consequently, my father would end up taking stuff he didn't need as payment for stuff his customers had charged, but didn't need.

Among the treasures Dad took to settle accounts were a live pig, a one-eyed Doberman, and a 1963 Dodge Dart. That car, which was white except for the red hood and blue passenger-side door, became my first set of wheels. It was the only reason I can think of that I couldn't land a date with any of the pretty girls in Smalltown until I was eighteen. That's when I traded up to a 1967 Chevy Nova, which wasn't fancy, but was all one color.

Raymond's Drugstore was three doors down from Smalltown IGA, and was a social center for townsfolk. It had a soda fountain with a counter and a dozen padded stools. I remember I could perch myself atop one of those stools and order, for a nickel, a soda custom-made from a variety of syrups mixed with soda water. My favorite was a cherry-grape-vanilla cola. For 24 cents, I could get a hot fudge sundae with whipped cream and nuts. The older people would sit for hours and nurse a 10-cent cup of coffee while discussing the details of how Reverend Campton's poodle got squashed by an eighteen-wheeler on Main Street, Tubby Ott's twelve-point buck, or the Widow Theriault's new boyfriend.

Station Street ends at Dan's Market, where Route 5 takes a hard right onto Main Street. Just around the corner from Dan's is beautiful Bandstand Park. As the creative name (the brainchild of a special "Come Up with a Clever Name for the Park" Subcommittee) implies, there is a gazebo-like bandstand smack-dab in the middle of the green. Every Wednesday night, from May until September, the park is the cultural center of town as the Smalltown Military Band takes to the bandstand and belts out tunes by the likes of John Philip Sousa and Scott Joplin. Children run in circles around the gazebo, teenagers flirt on park benches, and the older folks park their vehicles around the perimeter of the green and honk their horns in approval at the end of each rendition. This isn't the symphony or the opera, but it *is* part of our culture and traditions. It is good family entertainment, and far more wholesome than the New Moon Drive-in Theater down in St. Jamesboro, where many locals were conceived.

I guess we were a rather homogenous population when I was growing up in Smalltown. We had Catholics *and* Protestants, but that was about the extent of our ethnic diversity. I can remember only one black family and one Jewish family, but no one seemed to notice they were different. I can't recall a single person of Latino or Asian descent, though Mrs. Daley did have a Siamese cat.

Kids in Smalltown in the sixties stayed fairly fit. There were very few fatties. We were outside playing sports and hide-and-seek and "War." In the winter, we were out sledding, skiing, or playing in the snow. The houses were too crowded to keep all the little ankle-biters inside, so we were bundled up and sent out into the cold.

"Oh, Joey," Mom would say, "it's twenty-below outside—the warmest day we've had this week. Go out and play. You can come in when you can't feel your face anymore."

So, out we went. We'd build snow forts, throw snowballs at the girls, and sometimes toss our skis over one shoulder, our square-toed, leather ski boots over the other, and walk the mile or so to the Smalltown Outing Club. SOC was a big hill on the outskirts of town with two rope tows and a T-bar lift. It wasn't Vail or Stowe, but a kid could ski all day for 50 cents.

And why not. Our black-and-white TV got one channel on a good day, and it usually looked like the Lone Ranger and Tonto were riding their horses through a snowstorm in the desert. We had no computers, PlayStations, or Game Boys, so we went outside and burned calories.

Smalltown was blue-collar. Men and women worked in the Smalltown Tool & Die or Bag Balm factory, farmed, or earned their living in the woods. Most families had enough to get by, but kids found a way to earn their own spending money. I was a paperboy. I hauled forty-three copies of the *Smalltown News* around the village with a canvas bag over my shoulder or tucked into the basket of my Schwinn. On Fridays, I'd collect the weekly 42 cents for six papers from each of my customers. Of that 42 cents, I made 9 cents, so needless to say, my bank account grew quickly. I made enough to buy Christmas gifts for my family; I had spending money for the county fair; and I had a little left over for an occasional cherry-grape-vanilla cola at Raymond's Drugstore.

There wasn't much crime in Smalltown when I was a kid. There still isn't. We had a town cop back in the sixties. He wasn't someone to fear—he was a part of our community. He attended our church, his kids were our schoolmates; he was a friend. When I was twenty-one and foolish, he'd follow me to be sure I made it safely home after a night at Luigi's Lounge.

Smalltown was a wonderful place to grow up, and it's a great place to live today. Of course, living in a rural community is not without its challenges (see "Smalltown Life Ain't a Walk in the Park" and "The Stuff You See in People's Dooryards"). I've lived in this little town all my life (so far), and haven't ventured far from here very often. So naturally, my perspective on life and the world is that of an unworldly, backwoods bumpkin. I'm a simple guy trying, usually without success, to make sense of life in this modern world. I'm fairly certain my kids (among others) think I'm a clueless, unsophisticated stick-in-the mud, set in my ways, oblivious to reality, and stuck in the twentieth century.

While I'm sure I'm guilty of all of the above, I don't apologize for how I feel. Instead, I try to explain it. (See, for example, "Some Folks Shouldn't Wear Spandex" and "The World

Is Full of Stupid Drivers"). I've found I just cope better with things that annoy or confuse me if I write about them.

I hope this little tour of Smalltown helps you to better understand who I am and where I come from. Maybe now *Thoughts of an Average Joe* will make sense to you. Maybe you'll even agree with most of my thoughts. If not, well . . . I hate to say it . . . but you are just wrong.

Part I: Smalltown Life

Smalltown Life Ain't a Walk in the Park

I'VE ALWAYS BEEN GRATEFUL to have grown up in a small village. Smalltown is a good place to be from. It is nestled in the beautiful, rural, rugged mountains of the North Country, and offers a quiet, simple life where everybody knows your name.

That's not to say that Smalltown life is all peaches and cream. There are some downsides, like, it's rural, it's quiet, life is simple, and everybody knows your name.

There's a reason Smalltown isn't crowded. The winters are tough—although last year we got a break from Mother Nature, with only eight feet of snow. Besides, it stays above freezing for almost five months a year.

Sometimes the slow pace of Smalltown ain't all it's cracked up to be. "The simple life" is country-speak for "downright boring." There's not much in the way of fine dining in Smalltown. For that we have to travel more than twenty miles to the Buck & Doe Lodge in the town of Island Lake, which features venison specials on Wednesday nights following a poacher's moon.

You also have to drive a ways to take in some culture. Oh sure, there's Karaoke Night at Luigi's every Friday (people seem to flock from miles around to hear the little woman and me belt out our George Jones / Tammy Wynette repertoire), but movies are a different story. Two weeks ago, the little woman, Winnie, had a hankering to see a new movie. I had to drive her ten miles to the New Moon Drive-in Theater for some culture and french fries. I can see now why there was so much hoopla over *Titanic* at the 1997 Oscars.

I suppose it's nice to be raised in a place where everybody knows your name. It's no wonder, though. Heck, I'm related to half the people in town (probably more than that if I dug a little deeper into my genealogy, or followed up on the gossip of the town rumor mill). Most of us choose to ignore all that information. It's hard enough to find a date—say nothing about a wife—that isn't a cousin, as it is. Let's just say that some of the local family trees don't have all that many branches.

I can tell they have the same situation down the road in St. Jamesboro. Last summer, at the St. Jamesboro Rod & Gun Club cookout, Dizzy Dezell introduced me to his wife and cousin. (There was only one woman standing next to him.) Their little girl seemed cute enough, although her head looked to be a size too big for her body.

It's hard to get away with much in a town that's small. When I was nineteen, I walked into Dan's Market and confidently plopped a six-pack of Pabst Blue Ribbon, a $5 bill, and a fake ID on the checkout counter. I didn't know Mr. Hudson all that well, so I was surprised when he glanced at my doctored driver's license and said, "You ain't old enough to buy beer."

"What do you mean?" I protested. "It says right there I'm twenty-one."

"I don't care what this phony ID says. I know you was born in November, 1952, because I was up ta camp that year when your old man shot that ten-pointer. We had to stop to see you and your mother at the hospital on the way to the deer-reportin' station in St. Jamesboro." *Busted!*

To make things worse, because there isn't a boatload of excitement in our little hamlet, the *Smalltown News* reports every little event. When I was six years old, much to my mother's embarrassment, I made the newspaper when one of those two-for-a-penny Mint Julep candies down at Dan's found its way into the pocket of my dungarees. They couldn't name me in the paper, of course, but how many big-eared, eyeglasses-wearing, freckle-faced six-year-olds are there in a small town? Mom wasn't impressed, and I found it uncomfortable to sit for about a week thereafter.

My point is that Smalltown life ain't always a walk in the park. I'm so fed up with it, the little woman and I are thinking it's time to reach for the stars, see the world—maybe hook on the trailer and move up to Island Lake.

Small-Town Diners

SEEMS LIKE EVERY SMALL TOWN in America has at least one. It's a meeting place, a social center, a place where each day the problems of the town, the state, the country, and the world are solved—the local diner.

In some towns, it's a silver-sided, classic vestige of the 1950s, with a long row of vinyl-covered—often duct tape–patched—stools lined up at the Formica countertop, and eight or so booths, all with matching vinyl/duct-tape upholstery, along the opposite wall. At each booth is an antique remote control which, for a quarter, would play six of your favorite Elvis Presley, Buddy Holly, or Bobby Darin songs on the Wurlitzer. Now, of course, that same quarter will let you listen to any one of those same songs.

In other towns, the local diner / meeting place is not a stand-alone establishment, but part of a greater enterprise. It might be a part of the Pete's Exxon / General Store / Catering / Restaurant and Truck Rental. Or it could be the Bargain City Department Store and Café. Either way, locals are encouraged—no, expected—to weigh in on local, state, and national affairs.

Furthermore, if Pete has to run over to the checkout to sell a quart of milk and some roofing nails, customers are expected to help out with the cooking. I've seen it happen: "Jake, if you don't want your sausages to burn, you'd better get your lazy butt off that stool and flip 'em over while I go out and fill Effie's propane tank."

I like small-town diners, and I have some favorites along the routes to visit family or friends at various locations in northern New England. I've noticed the same characters at Pete's every time I'm there, regardless of time of day, and I'm sorry to say I'm guilty of eavesdropping on their conversations about the likes of Mary's latest child and boyfriend, or Percy's prostate surgery. Regulars hate to miss a day for fear they'll become the topic of conversation. Now, I don't visit family more than twice a year, but stopping at Pete's is like watching a TV soap opera. You can miss six months, tune in, and feel like you haven't skipped an episode.

I haven't figured out how the hardworking folks at those shiny little diners can turn a profit, serving the likes of Jake and his buddies a three-hour cup of coffee and a side of toast. They should replace the Wurlitzer remote control with a timing device, kind of like those used in taxicabs. The server would deliver the coffee, slap the timer, and move on to the next customer.

When Jake is ready to leave, he just slaps the timer, pays his $1.75 for his coffee and toast, and 5 cents a minute for booth rental. Standing up prior to inserting the proper coinage into the booth-rental machine would prompt the Wurlitzer to play a loud version of the Beatles's "I'm a Loser," and move the cheapskate's name to the top of the gossip list.

The Stuff You See in People's Dooryards

IT WASN'T UNTIL I LEFT northern New England for the first time that I realized most folks from other regions of the country have never heard of a dooryard.

Let me explain. A dooryard is that area outside the house where cars, trucks, snowmobiles, ATVs, and boats are parked, and any other junk is stored from which a man might need to cannibalize a part someday. The dooryard includes the driveway, the front lawn, and any other portion of the property that is needed to store such treasures as the broken-down 1973 Lawn-Boy riding tractor I'm keeping, just in case I might need the accelerator cable ten years from now.

My buddy Roy loves to ride around and see new places. Consequently, I've seen amazing dooryard collectibles. I've noticed satellite dishes have gotten a great deal smaller in the past ten years or so, but New Englanders are using the five-foot-wide black dish antennas of yesteryear for outdoor fire pits, flowerpots, and, most cleverly, as the roof of an outdoor gazebo.

Quite often, the value of the toys parked in a rural dooryard exceeds the value of the owner's house by 300 to 400 percent. Owners frequently spend far more for the heavy-duty silver tarps covering the Winnebago and the Boston Whaler than for the tattered, blue plastic cover on the house that has served to defer the need for new asphalt shingles for the past six years.

If you really want to see dooryard stuff, visit one of the island communities ten or more miles off the Maine coast. These islands are essentially very large rocks. There are no landfills or dumps, and it is cost-prohibitive for the fishing families who inhabit these rocks to ship their big junk to a landfill on the mainland. As a result, the dooryard of each cedar shake–covered home serves as a sort of museum of major household appliances. A 1950s vintage white Frigidaire with rounded corners and a single door might be wedged between its avocado-green, two-door replacement and a wringer washing machine.

Summer is the off-season for island fishermen, so their dooryards are adorned with piles of lobster traps, buoys, and rope, as well as marigolds growing in the satellite-dish planter.

As for the dooryard at the Wright estate in Smalltown, I like to keep it looking sharp . . . organized. I've parked all the lawn mowers together right next to the lineup of broken-down Ski-Doos, Skiroules, and Huskies, but separated from the rusty Massey Ferguson, the F-250 parts, and the various watercraft hulls.

I know my dooryard looks awesome, because after I mow around all my stuff, lots of folks stop to take pictures. I keep expecting to see a picture of my dooryard on one of those postcards depicting the scenic beauty of New England.

A Trip to the Dump

A TRIP TO THE TOWN DUMP ain't what it used to be. I'm old enough to remember the days when you could find the dump by following the smell of burning trash. There was a constant smudge going at the landfill, and that saved a lot of land from being filled. I suppose that wasn't so good for the ozone, but Al Gore was just a little kid then; we didn't know the glaciers were melting.

Going to the Smalltown dump as kids was part of our weekly entertainment in those days. Not only was there a big fire and a huge bulldozer to watch, but we never went without my .22 rifle, because there were always rats and crows to shoot. It was like going to the county fair, except there were no annoying "carnies" trying to steal my money: "Step right up. Three shots for a quartah heeah. Win the giant teddy bayuh." There was none of that; just me, my dad, my brothers, and hundreds of rodents. It was like one, giant, smelly, burning arcade.

I remember only one man working at the dump when I was a kid. Ernie was an old guy, or at least he seemed that way to a ten-year-old. He wore the same filthy overalls and T-shirt for twenty years. He was a scruffy-looking character; he never grew a real beard but always needed a shave. His two teeth were both brown, stained by the hundreds of pounds of Red Man chew he'd consumed over the years. I'm not sure how he chewed anything. His teeth, one on the top right, the other bottom left, didn't align well enough to be useful. I guess he gummed his food and tobacco.

Ernie wore a Red Sox ball cap with no brim. "Muh-muh-muh-muh-mistah muh-muh-muh-man," he'd stutter. "The fuh-fuh-fuh-first thing I do when I get a new hat is cut off the vizuh. Damned thing just gets in the wuh-wuh-wuh-wuh-way, and I'd be nuh-nuh-nuh-nuh-knockin' it off every fuh-fuh-fuh-five muh-muh-muh-muh-minutes."

Ernie was entertaining to a kid. He looked funny, talked funny, and drove an old Caterpillar bulldozer. What more could a boy want? His personal hygiene left a lot to be desired. I'm sure he smelled worse than the rats, but his scent was well concealed by the odor of burning rubbish.

There was no separating trash in those days—no recycling, reusing, or reducing. The cardboard and paper was burned with the leftover chicken, TV sets, and rubber tires. But you didn't have to worry about the fire spreading too far, because the town fathers had the foresight to build the dump near a bend in the river, which not only acted as a fire barrier but also carried all the toxins downstream toward our rivals in St. Jamesboro.

It's a lot more complicated going to the dump these days. There are special areas for recyclables—paper, glass, metal appliances, computer parts—and, of course, there's the landfill. There's a building there with a scale to drive onto so they can determine what your truck weighs, coming and going.

That scale got my buddy, Munzie, in big trouble one Saturday. It seems he made two trips to the landfill that day. He went once alone; the second time with his wife, Tiny, who wanted Munzie to take her to the "All You Can Eat Pancake Special" down at the Miss Smalltown Diner on the way home. Now, Tiny is a sweet woman, but she's not tiny—she's a "big-boned" lady.

There is something I should tell you about Munzie: He's never had an unspoken thought. So, on that particular Saturday morning, after he and his Silverado had been weighed for the second time (most recently with Tiny on board), he made the mistake of doing the math *aloud!*

"I didn't know you weighed two hundred and seven pounds," he told Tiny.

I'm pretty sure Munzie was the only guy at the diner that morning with a black eye.

Farmers and Flatlanders

MY BROTHER-IN-LAW Rick runs a dairy farm on the outskirts of Smalltown. He's a smart guy, and he and his wife Kassie have worked hard over the years. Theirs is one of the few dairy farms to have survived declining prices for bulk milk, the rising cost of feed, fuel, and equipment, and a poor economy.

Sherbert Hill, the site of the London Farm—where the little woman grew up, and where her brother still earns his living—is one of the prettiest areas I've ever laid eyes on. The views are incredible—*The Sound of Music* kind of views. Because of these scenic locations, many struggling farmers in northern New England have been able to sell their property to folks from away—flatlanders—for a tidy profit.

One such flatlander, William Fitzpatrick, bought the Johnson farm just up the road from Rick's place a few years back. He travels from New York to visit his new property for about two weeks each summer. Rick cuts the hay from his fields and keeps an eye on the place in William's absence. Rick likes William, and finds his new neighbor's flatlander ways entertaining.

One day last summer, William stopped at Rick's place to ask a favor.

"Sorry to be a bother, Rick, but I noticed you have some *Asclepias tuberosa* growing in the meadow by the barn."

"I have what?" Rick asked.

"*Asclepias* . . . you know, milkweed," William explained. "I was wondering if you'd mind if I get some milk from your milkweed."

Rick laughed. "I don't think that'll work out for ya, William, but you're welcome to try."

"Thank you, Rick; you're a swell neighbor."

Rick's sides were hurting from laughter as he told Kassie the latest flatlander story.

Not a half-hour later, William was back at the door with a quart jug of milk in hand. "Just wanted to thank you for the milk, Rick. Mrs. Fitzpatrick and I will enjoy it on our cereal in the morning."

"Uhhh, umm, okay . . . You're welcome." Rick was confused and nearly speechless.

Three days later William stopped by the barn, where Rick and Kassie were doing their daily chores. "Excuse me, Rick, but I spotted some *Lonicera periclymenum* down in your lower pasture. Would you mind terribly if I gathered a small jar of honey from that lovely honeysuckle patch I saw down there?"

"Heck no, William—knock yourself out."

"Oh, thank you, Rick. I appreciate your generosity."

Rick shook his head and grinned at Kassie, who rolled her eyes in disbelief as the foolish flatlander walked away.

The following day, William returned with a jar of pure honey in hand. "Hello, Rick. Just wanted to thank you for the honey. While I was at it, I gathered a jar for you and Kassie. Seemed like the least I could do."

"That's a good one, William," Rick chuckled, taking the honey from his neighbor. "Thank you."

A week had passed when Rick answered the doorbell at his farmhouse to find William on his doorstep. "Afternoon, William."

"Good afternoon, Rick. Say, neighbor, were you aware that you have some *Amaryllis belladonna* down in your Quimby Field?"

"All right, William, I'll bite. What is it I've got growin' down in the Quimby field?"

"*Amaryllis belladonna* . . . Maybe you know them as Naked Ladies?"

My brother-in-law abruptly interrupted his flatlander neighbor. "Hang on, William—I'll grab my jacket and go with you."

Crazy like a Fox

EVERY SMALL TOWN has at least one eccentric, old "crazy person" who lives alone, seems to be without friends or family, isn't big on personal hygiene (stinks), and is looked down upon by the more fortunate townsfolk.

When I was a younger man, Smalltown was home to several such characters, one of whom was Dick Jenkins. Dick lived in a run-down, two-room shack he'd built on a hillside in the 1930s. He'd venture into the village and into the Smalltown IGA (my dad's store) once a month, a day or two after his check from the government arrived. Dad liked him, but also liked to make Dick's visits to our store as brief and efficient as possible. (He smelled wicked bad.) Dick's essence was hard to describe—a stale combination of body odor, wood smoke, cat urine, and bad breath.

Dad's strategy for moving Dick expeditiously through Smalltown IGA was to assign me as Dick's personal shopping assistant. The bad news was that I had to spend about twenty minutes with Stinky Dick Jenkins. The good news was that I got to listen to his stories and get to know the amazing man inside the dirty, foul-smelling exterior.

As a twenty-year-old, it was my job and (despite the odor) my pleasure to guide Dick through the IGA, dropping cans of baked beans, a block of cheddar cheese, and frozen, reduced-price hamburger into his cart while listening to his colorful, expletive-laced stories.

Dick would laugh and tell me how he'd sold his land—twenty acres on a beautiful hillside, with a view of the valley to die for—to a New York lawyer when Dick was seventy-two and seemingly on his last leg. He'd insisted on a clause that allowed him to live out his life on that land without any new neighbors. He was eighty-nine when he told me, "All my friends are dead. They drank water from the faucet. I get mine right off the #$@%*& roof! That's why I don't get sick!"

In the 1960s, Dick became a sort of folk hero to some of the freethinking, long-haired, young, hippie wannabes. I knew some of them fairly well, and can tell you they didn't smell much better than old Dick. He told me the State Police came to his door one day asking questions about his young friends.

"They asked me if I'd seen them rascals usin' drugs." I remember how he grinned, exposing a few tobacco-stained teeth. "I told the cops they was crazy. Them kids can't afford no drugs! Hell, they're so poor, they sit on my floor and pass around the same cigarette!" I knew that Dick knew better, and I'm sure the police did, too.

Dick Jenkins died in 1981, at ninety-one. I was sad that day, and sorry that most of the folks in Smalltown never knew Dick the way I did. I'm glad I got to know the bright, funny man, who'd fought for his country, lost his family in an awful fire in 1928, and worked hard to eke out a living, hauling logs with his horses, Jake and Pete.

Most of the folks in town knew Dick as the stinky, old, crazy man—the "fool on the hill." They didn't realize he'd lived his life happily, on his own terms, in a house he'd built with his own hands on one of the most picturesque spots in northern New England, sold it for a fair chunk of change, living there rent-free for the last nineteen years of his life . . . a fool indeed.

I Like Beer

I LIKE BEER. BEER IS GOOD. There's nothing like a cold beer on a hot summer day, or a cold winter night, or . . . well, you get the idea.

Beer drinking has become more complicated than when I started drinking it in the late sixties. Back then, there were about six kinds: Bud, Schlitz, Miller, Schaefer, Pabst, and Narragansett. There were probably others; they just didn't have them at the Smalltown IGA, Dan's Market, or Luigi's Lounge. Nowadays, there's a microbrewery in every county making "designer beer." I'm not a big fan of those fancy brews. Beer shouldn't taste like pumpkins or blueberries or lemons or chocolate. Beer should taste like . . . well . . . beer.

The best thing to happen to my favorite beverage in the past forty years is diet beer. I'm a bit of a health nut, so if I'm going to enjoy a dozen or more brewskis, it's got to be Bud Light. That's why the waist size on my Levi's hasn't changed in twenty years, though I do wear them a few inches lower these days. The little woman, Winnie, is concerned that my legs are shrinking because my jeans have gone from a size 36/31 to 36/27 since I met her. I think they just make them different now.

This is a true story (the names have been changed to protect the guilty). My buddy Munzie's favorite beer is O.P.

(Other People's). The year I met him, he was having trouble seeing eye to eye with his (now former) wife, so he spent nearly every evening at my house watching the Sox or the Pats and drinking my Bud Light. I enjoyed his company, so I was happy to share my beer. I'd just ask Winnie to pick up an extra case or so at the IGA every week.

Roughly a year (fifty-two cases of Bud Light) later, we all went camping. Another friend, Barney, offered to make a beer run, so I ordered myself a case. Munzie ordered a case, too.

"Bud Light?" Barney asked.

I was quite surprised at Munzie's reply. "Oh, no thanks," he replied. "I don't really like that kind."

I wasn't upset with Munzie—just grateful I didn't stock the flavor he likes. Lord knows how many more cases I'd have gone through.

Barney likes to drink beer, too—lots of beer. His beer-consumption philosophy is: "If you weren't supposed to drink thirty (or more) beers a day, they wouldn't make thirty-packs." He doesn't believe thirty-packs were made to share with friends. Barney's the only guy I know with a padlock on his beer cooler. I think that's in large part because of Munzie's preference for O.P., and the philosophy of another mutual friend, Roy, who likes to say: "You can't drink beer all day if you don't start in the morning."

In our younger years, it was fairly easy to tell how many "wobbly pops" Barney had enjoyed by the looks of the girl he was dancing with. It seems that all the young ladies at Rex's Dance Hall got a little prettier with each beer. I hate to say it, but some of the twenty-beer women were homelier than a mud fence.

Barney Lang is a five-foot-six-inch scrawny wimp until he has about a dozen beers. Then he's six and a half feet of muscle . . . and mouth. It's at about that time of the night when he finds the homely girl with the biggest boyfriend and makes his move.

If I had a cold beer for every time I got my butt kicked for knowing Barney, I'd have enough O.P. to supply Munzie for another year.

Need Directions? Get Lost!

IT'S HARD TO GET good directions. Last October, I was upcountry and asked a local where I might find some partridges (yeah, I know there are no partridges up there). But, ask about grouse, and you're sure to be instantly labeled as "one of them highbrows from downcountry."

Anyway, Alton, at the Lincoln Mobil Station, gave me very detailed directions as I pumped my own gas. "If it's birds you're lookin' for, you wanna go to the Bent Culvert Road over to Loon Lake. Just take this here road 'til it almost ends, then keep goin' about two, two and a half miles."

I was having some trouble following Alton's directions, especially since I was so distracted by the Swisher Sweets cigarillo he never removed from between his lips. He held it dead center in his mouth, and it bounced like a maestro's baton during the "William Tell Overture."

"Yessah, just about a quarter-mile before you get to a wicked sharp right-hand curve, you take a left on the Bent Culvert Road, then you go to the Y in the road, and take that left. Don't take the right, 'cause that ain't where the birds are. Good deer huntin' out there, though. My uncle Royce shot a ten-pointer out there in '67—ain't no birds, though."

After about five minutes, I was wondering how long that cigarillo could burn, and how much brain damage does one suffer when his only fresh air is inhaled during sleeping hours.

I thanked Alton, and off I went in search of the Y on the Bent Culvert Road.

Three hours later, I was back at the Lincoln Mobil Station with 120 more miles on my truck, no birds, and no clue about the location of the Bent Culvert Road. I explained that I had taken this road two and a quarter miles past where it almost ends, and the only left—which was indeed a quarter-mile before a sharp right curve—was marked with a sign that read Norton Trail Road.

Alton, sucking on a fresh cigarillo, replied, "Yup, you found it. The State calls it Norton Trail Road, but that ain't its real name. That's the Bent Culvert Road. Any birds out there?"

I rubbed my face with my hand. "I don't know."

"You took the left at the Y, didn't ya? 'Cause they ain't no birds to the right, just an old culvert that was stove up by a loggin' truck."

"Yup, I took the left," I lied. "Just no birds today. Maybe I'll come back in November and go to the right to look for deer."

Alton's cigarillo danced again as he offered more assistance. "Well, stop in then, and I'll tell you how to get to Bald Archie's Cutoff. It ain't but three miles this side of the Five Corners on Lost Indian Trail."

I could still see Alton's cigarillo bouncing and his flailing hands pointing out directions as I glanced in my rearview mirror and headed for home. I made a mental note to myself: *Pick up new DeLorme and GPS.*

Outhouses Have Come a Long Way

I GREW UP AT A TIME when every camp—and these were camps, not cottages—had an outhouse. My grandparents built a camp on a small pond up north in the 1940s. The outhouse was named Myra. As far as I know, the moniker had no significance, but I've since wondered if my grandmother had an unpopular neighbor by the same name.

These days most "camps" have running water and indoor plumbing, but at festivals, outdoor weddings, and construction sites, we get to occasionally revisit the outhouse in the form of the plastic portable toilet.

I like the brand names given to these modern-day privies: Porta-John, Port-O-let, Johnny on the Spot, Porta-Potty . . . Some of the companies that supply and service the plastic portables have come up with some catchy marketing slogans, too. "We're #1 in the #2 Business" is one of my favorites, although I think "Heeere's Johnny" is quite clever, too.

Most people seem to have a favorite Porta-John story. Mine involves the little woman, Winnie. We were in Nova Scotia at a music festival a few years back, and, because we had chosen not to haul our little aluminum love shack on wheels all the way up to Halifax, we were without bathroom facilities of our own. Winnie hates public toilets, so she hovers (whatever that means).

As it turns out, Canada has more stringent Porta-John regulations than the United States. For each bank of plastic privies, there has to be at least one hand-wash station, which consists of a separate polyurethane cube, each side of which has a built-in soap dispenser and a water supply operated by a foot pump.

The little woman and I were washing up, and I mentioned how impressed I was with the hand-wash station when Winnie came out with it. "It's a great idea, but I don't understand why they need these when there is that cute little sink with the little round bar of pink soap right beside the toilet in the Porta-John."

I didn't mean to laugh so hard, and I can honestly say that I regretted it, especially since for the remainder of the weekend, I sported a shiner and swollen left eyelids.

The good news is that when you share a story like that (and it would be a shame to keep such a story to yourself), you hear similar stories. The promoter of the music festival shared that his all-time favorite comment received on a post-festival survey form was from a New Brunswick lady who wrote, "The festival site was spotless and the facilities were excellent. I particularly liked the little bin in the Porta-John because I never know what to do with my pocketbook when I'm in there. Thanks—Monique."

Winnie swears she didn't use the sink or the little pink soap, and I believe her. I also believe she's thankful for Monique.

Potholes and Frost Heaves

THE SNOW AND ICE OF WINTER make for some treacherous driving at times, and if you've driven on New England roads for long, you've probably been scared to the point of incontinence while behind the wheel. There's nothing to get your juices flowing like the helpless feeling of doing repeated 360-degree turns while crossing an icy bridge. Still, I think I prefer the ice and snow of winter to the potholes and frost heaves of spring.

Asphalt doesn't hold up well to six months of frozen precipitation and the plowing, sanding, and salting required to keep New England roads passable. I live near the top of Winding Hill Road, and by late March, the daily commute is like a roller coaster on a slalom course. Any chance of avoiding significant damage to the suspension and front-end alignment of my truck is dependent upon my ability to avoid cavernous potholes and anticipate those sometimes-significant heaves in the pavement caused by expanding frost.

I'm not too quick these days, so I try to wait at my driveway for a younger driver—one that isn't talking on a cell phone—to pass by. I'll then follow them at a safe distance. This system works fairly well. I follow their course down the hill until they hit a pothole, which I then know to avoid.

My buddy, Wilbur Gilliam, is a mountain of a man. He's not fat; he's got a lot of muscle on his bones. He's also cross-eyed . . . and he's cheap. When gasoline prices rose above four bucks a gallon, Wilbur bought a used Mini Cooper. Did you ever take a good look at the front end of a Mini Cooper? The way the headlights and grille are arranged, it looks like a face. It sort of grimaces at you like it's burdened with the task of hauling its owner around—understandable in Wilbur's case. Wilbur in his Cooper was quite a sight to behold. I've opened sardine cans that weren't so tightly packed.

Driving the springtime obstacle course has always been a greater challenge for Wilbur than for most, because of the crooked eye. His depth perception is . . . well . . . he doesn't have any. You'd think he would hit about half of the potholes but, for some reason, he averages hitting about 90 percent.

One April morning on my way to the dump, I could see that the traffic in the oncoming lane was moving slowly to avoid a small car and a huge man. It seems that Wilbur had planted the right front tire of his Cooper so deeply into a very large pothole that he'd broken a tie rod, the right headlight was dangling, and he'd lost his dentures.

I, of course, pulled over to see if I could help, and as I approached, Wilbur stood next to his car and grinned, exposing his toothless piehole. I didn't mean to laugh so hard. I just couldn't help myself.

When I regained my composure, Wilbur asked, "What's so damned funny?"

"I'm sorry, buddy, but with that crooked headlight and black grille, your car looks just like you!"

Luckily, Wilbur has been a friend for a long time and isn't thin-skinned, or he might have rearranged my grille to match his and his car's.

It occurs to me that there are no potholes or frost heaves on a well-built, well-maintained, gravel road. I'm considering proposing legislation to ban the use of asphalt on any road or highway north of Massachusetts.

The Demolition Derby at Dan's Market

BIG PARKING LOTS drive me crazy. It doesn't seem to matter whether it's the lot at Dan's Market or Small-Mart; they all scare the bejeebers out of me. There are more rules, and more careful drivers, in a demolition derby at the county fair. On the roads and highways, most drivers know, and follow, the laws and rules of etiquette; but turn into a shopping center parking lot and it's every person for themselves.

Last week, I drove the little woman over to Dan's to pick up some grub. I love to eat, but I hate grocery stores, so I waited in the truck and took in the greatest show on earth. It's like watching extreme fighting, but without the rules that prohibit things like eye gouging, biting, or throat punches. Heck, I can sit in the supermarket parking lot for free and watch folks—many of whom I also see kneeling piously at church on Sunday mornings—treating one another with total disrespect and ill will.

My favorite show on that particular day was the soccer mom in the brand-new Volvo station wagon who slowly cruised the lot—up Row A, down Row B, then diagonally across the empty spots at the end of Row B to get to Row C. Around and around, prowling like a coyote, waiting to pounce on a spot near the store entrance. I watched her cruise for ten minutes—and then it happened. A red Chevy backed slowly out of its spot as an elderly couple waited patiently, in their thirty-foot Mercury Grand Marquis, to take its place. The Chevy was barely out of her way when Sally Soccer Mom pulled across the lane to cut in front of the old folks, nearly scraping the GIVE PEACE A CHANCE sticker off the bumper of her Volvo.

The senior citizens and I watched in disbelief as Sally jumped out of her car, her Gucci exercise outfit still damp with perspiration following her sixty-minute Tae Bo workout at the Ladies Fitness Center, and walked the few yards to the grocery store, pleased to have saved herself that extra twenty or so steps from the empty spots at the end of Row B. In spite of my wishes, she made it into the store without getting tire tracks on her overstuffed designer outfit.

It seems to me that most of these parking lots are not designed with pickup trucks in mind. The rows are too close together, and the spaces too narrow, to allow for my F-150 to back out and turn to exit in a single maneuver.

That's a big part of the reason I'd rather go to the oral surgeon than shop. I'm telling you, current parking lot designs discourage shopping by pickup truck owners. With that in mind, I've been thinking I could save money by trading the little woman's Honda Civic for a brand-new three-quarter-ton F-250 with a crew cab, dualies, and an eight-foot bed.

The Great Brandon Fire of 1999

FOR NEARLY TWENTY YEARS, I've played bluegrass music with friends, most of whom live in southern Maine. In the early 1990s, we formed a band, Basic Bluegrass, which has toured internationally (we played in Canada once). Basic Bluegrass includes my friend Walt on banjo, Munzie and Roy on guitars, Warren on Dobro, and Barney thumping the stand-up bass. I play the mandolin.

One of the band's most memorable weekends occurred in March 1999, when we played to a sellout crowd at the Neshobe Sportsmen's Club's annual Spaghetti Feed and Bluegrass Show in Brandon, Vermont. I think there were more folks there for the spaghetti than for the music. There were a lot of "big" fans there, if you know what I mean.

The show ended at eleven o'clock, and it was pushing midnight by the time we tore down and packed up. Barney and I were back at the Honey Dew Motel and Miniature Golf Resort at 12:30. The rest of the band and entourage hadn't returned by 1:30 a.m., and we were so worried we decided to drink another beer and wait up for them.

Finally, at 1:45, they arrived and told us the story of what has come to be known as "The Great Brandon Fire of 1999." This story is mostly true with hardly any exaggeration (honest). It seems that after leaving the Neshobe Sportsmen's Club, Munzie astutely noticed a small house with smoke billowing from its

large center chimney. He pulled over and flagged down Warren, who was following him and had a cellular phone.

Munzie, an excitable guy, spoke faster than the guy on
the Viagra commercials—you know, the one who lists all the
dreadful, potential side effects.

"Slow down, Munzie," Warren pleaded. "I can't hear that fast."

Munzie said he would, but didn't. "That house is on fire—
smoke pourin' out the top, and there's people in there just
drinkin' coffee like they don't even know their house is burnin'.
Call 911! Glo just ran down to warn the people inside."

Walt grabbed the phone and called Chief Frank Stevens of
the Brandon Volunteer Fire Department.

"I want to report a fire," Walt said.

"Sir, where is the fire?" Chief Stevens asked.

"I don't know."

"You don't know?"

"Well, I mean, I'm not from around here, and I don't know
where I am, but there's a house afire. It's in Brandon, and
there's a big blue house just up the road."

"Sir, I'm going to need more information than that."

"Warren, drive up the road a piece and see if we come to a
crossroads," Walt suggested.

"Good thinking," Stevens said.

"We're comin' up to an intersection. We're on Old County
Road and the crossroad is Meadow Road."

"Okay, sir, I know about where you are," Stevens
responded. "I'll get our trucks right out there. Go back to the
scene so you can flag us down."

Meanwhile, Glo, Munzie's girlfriend, had tried to run down the hill to the house, but had slipped on the glare ice and slid on her backside until her feet slammed against the door with a thud loud enough to get the attention of the folks inside, one of whom answered the door. Glo scrambled like a three-legged dog playing fetch on a frozen lake, trying to right herself, and issued her frantic warning.

"There's smoke pourin' out the top of your house," she exclaimed, already imagining her photo, accepting the Mayor's Award for Valor, on the front page of the *Brandon News.*

"It's supposed to be like that . . . but thanks," the lady at the door replied, calmly sipping her coffee.

The conversation was interrupted by the wailing sirens and flashing red lights of fire trucks and an ambulance, which were only slightly more distracting than the screaming and arm-flailing antics of Bobby Jo and Pammy, Walt and Warren's women.

I'm happy to report there were no serious injuries suffered as a result of the "Big Fire"; only a mild concussion suffered by Chief Stevens, upon his arrival at the scene, as a result of repeatedly banging his head against the steering wheel of his truck while laughing and yelling, "A sugarhouse! I can't believe it—a maple sugarhouse!"

Basic Bluegrass has played in Brandon, Vermont, several times since "The Great Fire," but for some reason, we (or any other southern Maine band, for that matter) have never been invited for a repeat performance in February or March.

Going Postal

GROWING UP IN A SMALL TOWN, I visited the post office nearly
every day. Our family lived in the village; home mail delivery
was not an option, so I picked up the mail every day on my
way home from school at lunchtime. Yup, I walked to and
from Smalltown Elementary—nearly three miles each way,
most of it uphill—four times a day, in a part of the world
where the temperature hovered around zero for half the year.
Okay, so maybe I've embellished a bit, but let's just say the
walk was far enough that there weren't many fat kids in my
seventh-grade class.

The post office was an important social center in our little
village. Since nearly everyone had a post office box, most
townsfolk stopped by every day or two. They planned their
daily mail pickup to be at a certain time—in part because they
knew someone else who would make that same pickup time
part of their daily routine. Lots of local news was disseminated
in that post office lobby. It was important stuff, like the young
widow, Cindy Peterson, dating Bucky Simons within days
of his release from prison. And to think it had been only six
months since her late husband's tragic human catapult experi-
ment. The word at the post office was that his last words were,
"Cindy, watch this!"

I still live in Smalltown, but on the outskirts now, and a
mailman drives to my mailbox and delivers a bill or two and

several pieces of junk mail six days a week. Most of the mail
I receive is for me or a family member, but I must say I've
learned a lot about my neighbors through receiving mail
intended for their mailbox. If not for my inept, careless mail
delivery person, I'd have no clue that old Mr. Gotlowski still
likes to look at pictures of naked women. It was fun delivering
that magazine to him personally. It may have been a week late
and slightly dog-eared, but the way his face flushed, I could
tell he was pleased to finally receive it.

There isn't a mailbox in my neighborhood that hasn't fallen
victim to the snowplow. Sometimes, on my way to work, following an overnight blizzard, it's like maneuvering my pickup
truck through a slalom course of fallen mailboxes. One particularly snowy winter, every one of my neighbors had to use
the old mailbox post in the five-gallon bucket of sand trick
in order to receive postal deliveries for the remainder of the
winter. Three years later, Mr. Gotlowski still uses that system.
No sense in rushing into a permanent fix—especially with so
many magazines to read (or, at least, look at).

Did I mention that, since 2002, I have not lost a mailbox
to the evil snowplow driver? Well, that's a fact. I picked my
mailbox up off the street three times that winter and I'd had
enough. This was war! I live on a cul-de-sac, which Zeke
plows in both directions, giving him two ways to knock down
my postal hardware—trust me, he got me coming and going.

You've heard that necessity is the mother of invention.
Well, Zeke was the mother that inspired my invention of
the Snowplow Buster Mailbox System. The SBMS is very

low-tech: a board, two washers, a nut, and a bolt. It swings both ways (something I've accused Zeke of more than once).

After the first few storms of the winter of 2003, I found my mailbox dislocated left twice, and once to the right, but still intact. Zeke hasn't hit it since. The contest is over; Zeke seems disinterested in playing a game he can't win. He still attacks my neighbors, though—even knocks down Mr. Gotlowski's sand-bucket post sometimes. Being a good neighbor, I'm always there to right his mailbox, gather up his letters and magazines, and—eventually—deliver them to his door.

I Just Love Mud Season

HERE IN NORTHERN NEW ENGLAND, we wait all winter for the next season—Mud Season. By late April, I am sick and tired of snow and cold, and ready for some warmer weather. It's not a pretty time of year; it's the season of sand-covered roads, dirty snowbanks, and gray, rain-filled skies. There are leaves to rake, limbs and branches to pick up, and broken trees to knock down and saw into firewood. There's a winter's worth of sand to power-broom off the lawn and back into the street as blackflies attack every square millimeter of exposed skin and invade every orifice.

I start preparing in November for Mud Season, when the sun starts gaining strength, the days lengthen, and, consequently, the ground starts to soften. Each fall, I push little white plastic dowels topped with baseball-size red reflectors every eight feet or so along the edge of my asphalt driveway to help my friend, Barney, who plows my dooryard, remember its bends and boundaries.

By mid-December every year, it becomes clear to me that Barney views my strategically placed reflectors as targets. He, unfortunately, is more accurate with his Fisher plow blade than with his deer rifle. So, by January, the little woman and I are driving with two tires on asphalt, and two on the lawn we spend six to seven months each year manicuring to resemble the fairways at Pebble Beach. After February, the ground starts to soften, so you can probably imagine the condition of the sod along the edges of my driveway after Barney plows, following a mid-March snowstorm. I can tell Barney feels bad about the condition of my lawn each spring because it is reflected in the bill he sends each April: "Plowing—2 storms: $50. Landscaping: no charge."

I get itchy each April to get up to camp. After a long winter, I'm anxious to get the place opened up for spring fishing. The road into camp is about a mile of hard-packed dirt with a sprinkling of gravel on the surface. Every April, Winnie and I load up the old F-150 with the tools we'll need to repair the damages inflicted by Mother Nature over the winter, along with just enough provisions to get us through a weekend, and head north.

It seems to be the same every year. The first quarter-mile, which is plowed by Roscoe Leonard—who lives year-round on the camp road—is a bit muddy but well enough traveled to get us to the stretch of road that winds its way through the woods to our little piece of heaven.

It happened again this April. I drove the pickup in past Roscoe's place and jumped out to remove the padlock from the cable I stretch across the camp road, each winter, to keep trespassers from stealing my $5 Zebco fishing rod or the little woman's velvet Elvis picture.

As always, I walked up and down the road a bit to test it for firmness. After jumping up and down a few times, I proclaimed it as passable. "Look, dear—it ain't budgin' under my hundred and seventy pounds."

"What about the other thirty pounds?" Winnie inquired. The little woman is hilarious. "That's what you said last year. Are you sure? 'Cause I don't want to go through that again!"

Anyway, a half-hour later Roscoe is there with his John Deere, ready to haul my F-150 out of the mud for the fourth April in a row.

"Figured you'd be needin' me 'bout now. There's a lot of frost in the ground this time of year . . . every year," he grinned. Seems like everybody's a comedian.

It was painful handing $40 over to Roscoe, but I knew it wouldn't hurt near as much as the fourth annual "I Told You So" tongue-lashing I was about to endure when I climbed into my truck for the long ride home.

Bicycles Have Changed Since I Was a Kid

BICYCLES HAVE CHANGED since I was a kid. My first bike was a twenty-four-inch Schwinn—a real beauty that I was proud of. She was black with shiny chrome fenders. It was a boy's bike, which in those days meant there was a bar running essentially from the handlebars to the seat. Thinking back, considering the pain that ensued when the chain slipped, I'm not so sure that bar should have been on a boy's bike.

I couldn't ride that first bike when I got it. Dad had to teach me how. I remember him running along beside me as I tried to summon all the coordination my six-and-a-half-year-old body could muster. It was a struggle. Pedaling, steering, and balancing—all at once.

"Don't let go, Daddy," I yelled as I pedaled and wobbled down Eastern Street.

"I won't let go, Joey, I promise," he lied.

Before I knew it, I was on my own. "I'm doing it, Daddy! I can ride by myself! Uh-oh . . . Whoa!" *Crash.* "Daddy, you let go! You promised!"

Dad knew what he was doing. In half a day I was indeed pedaling, steering, and balancing—all on my own.

Once I got the hang of riding my bike, I was unstoppable. It was like having my own Harley. I even tried to duplicate the sound of a motorcycle by clothes-pinning baseball cards to my front sprocket in such a way that they'd rub against the spokes of my wheel and make a noise that mildly resembled that of a Harley. I've recently discovered that the noise of those Roberto Clemente and Sandy Koufax cards in my spokes was the same sound made by Derek Jeter and A-Rod cards running through my paper shredder today.

As boys tend to do, I grew, and at twelve, I became an entrepreneur. I had a paper route. Consequently, I needed a new bike. Santa brought me a new Schwinn—a twenty-six-inch beast with all the bells and whistles. It was the two-wheel equivalent of a sixties vintage Cadillac Coupe de Ville. The fenders were chrome, again. Where the boy's bar was, it had a compartment for batteries. It looked sort of like the gas tank on a Harley. There were headlights, a horn, multicolored plastic streamers coming out of the handgrips, and, in the back, baskets for the forty-three copies of the *Smalltown News* I delivered daily. It had one speed . . . slow . . . especially if I was pedaling uphill.

Bikes are much different these days. They have twenty speeds and shock-absorbent titanium frames. There are special outfits: tight-fitting fluorescent spandex with special padding to cushion the ride. And helmets are a must. We never wore helmets to ride a bike. To do so would have meant verbal and physical abuse far more devastating than the few head-to-tree or asphalt injuries I endured on my Schwinn. Besides, those head injuries helped make me what I am today.

A True Friend Is Hard to Find

I'VE TURNED A LOT OF PAGES on the calendar (over 700), and
with each passing month I further appreciate the value of a
true friend. They're hard to come by, and for reasons I don't
understand, I've been blessed with several.

A true friend overlooks, sometimes admires, your short-
comings. He'll say things like, "That was a corker, Joe—you
cleared the room! Musta been the baked beans and deer liver
you ate up ta camp last night."

When you've spent thousands of hours of quality time with
a friend, there's no need to tell jokes. The catalog of funny
stories shared and repeated for each new visitor at camp is
immense. In the absence of new blood, all that is required are
punch lines. I can bring rib-cage pain to my closest buddies by
saying, "Aggravatin', ain't it?," or cause beer to spew out their
noses by repeating, "She didn't look like no cop, did she?"
Punch-line humor is a real time-saver, which is really important to a group of busy overachievers like my pals and me.

A good buddy doesn't bail you out of jail because, if he's a
real friend, he'll be right there in the cell beside you, saying,
"You're right, Joe, those biker chicks put up a better fight than
the cops, but maybe you shouldn't have mentioned that to
Deputy Stevens."

A little north of Smalltown, there's a dance hall where I
spent a good many Saturday nights as a younger man. Mo's

is a bring-your-own-beverage establishment, which typically features a country band and a rowdy crowd. Its patrons are the industrious loggers, farmers, carpenters, and factory workers of the North Country. They work hard all week and let loose on Saturday night.

As if a rowdy crowd, cheap drinks, and a country band were not enough to incite trouble, Mo's typically features a dance that ensures a man will be paired up to slow-dance with another man's lady. The band declares a "Paul Jones" by playing an up-tempo song like "Turkey in the Straw" and announcing "Ladies on the inside, gentlemen on the outside." The two circles of alcohol-fueled participants orbit in opposite directions until the music stops, at which time the fella grabs onto the gal in front of him and dances to a waltz number until he hears "Turkey in the Straw" again, and the process is repeated.

Once, back in the eighties, my brother-in-law Rick and I were walking off the dance floor after a Paul Jones marathon, and he told me, "Joe, I think I just set a world record. I danced with a ton of women in just eight minutes!" I laughed, and we agreed that the Mo's crowd was a particularly rough bunch that night. "I'm a little scared, Rick," I said. "I'm thinkin' if it weren't for incest, we might be here alone."

Around midnight, I heard the band strike up "Turkey in the Straw" again, and knew this couldn't end well. But my friend Jim Beam convinced me I should join in the fun. As luck would have it, I landed across from the same big-boned woman twice in a row. On the second encounter, she muckled on to me like she meant business; I was having trouble breathing. "Turkey in the Straw" had become my new favorite song, but when I heard it, big Sylvia wouldn't let go. As it turns out, letting my body go limp and playing dead didn't work with Sylvia, like it reportedly does with a grizzly bear.

Sylvia's man, Lester, was 300 pounds of Budweiser-infused muscle, and didn't like what he was seeing. "Let go of my Sylvie!" he demanded.

"I'm trying to, buddy. She won't let me!"

Lester didn't want to hear that.

"I said, let go of her . . . now!"

Sylvia, apparently hell-bent on making Lester jealous and ending my life in the process, tightened her embrace. I was, to this rugged woman, like a T-bone to a Doberman; she wasn't about to let go. Lester was on the verge of committing homicide when Rick, being a true friend, came to my rescue. He wedged himself between me and the enraged giant, looked squarely into Lester's bulging, vein-engorged eyes, and came to my defense.

"Mister, he's not trying to steal your woman. I can tell you, for sure, Joe don't even *like* fat women." And that's when the trouble escalated.

So, there we were, Lester, Rick, and me, sharing a jail cell and wondering why Sylvia was out there free on a Sunday morning enjoying pancakes, bacon, and donuts over at the Miss Smalltown Diner, while Rick and I couldn't even think of eating.

In friendship, I guess all's well that ends well. Rick's fat lip and facial swelling resolved in about a week, and my new front teeth look almost like the originals.

Them Damned Hippies

"THEM DAMNED HIPPIES!"

I must have heard that a thousand times growing up. It was Smalltown in the 1960s, and thousands of free-spirited young people were fleeing the big cities to commune with nature in this rural, peaceful, beautiful place my family called home.

As you might expect, there was often strife between the two factions of Smalltown residents. The natives were conservative farmers, loggers, and laborers who believed that every able-bodied person should pull their own weight, and that this is America—love it or leave it. "You damned hippies."

On the other hand, the new immigrants were left-leaning peaceniks who hated the establishment and felt America's wealth should be shared equally by all, regardless of brains, talent, or level of effort. "Damned, lazy hippies."

The tree-hugging, long-haired liberals hated the loggers and the beef farmers who, in turn, despised the tofu-loving flower children. It was downright ugly at times. You may be wondering why I'm stirring up this conflict between the rational-minded Smalltown natives and those crazy damned hippies. It's essentially because the little woman, Winnie, grew up on a dairy farm on the outskirts of Smalltown. Her parents worked harder and smarter than most, and made a good living on the farm, back when a family could. Winnie's brother Rick and his wife Kassie still run the farm and are doing well because they were wise enough to see the writing on the wall and worked hard to jump through all the government hoops in order to allow their farm to become certified organic.

Now, they produce organic milk, beef, eggs, turkeys, chickens, and vegetables, and feature those organic products at their restaurant in downtown Smalltown. The organic food tastes better, and is more healthful, yet Rick and Kassie frequently hear complaints about it. "I don't want that damned hippie food," said Zeke, from the Smalltown Body Shop.

"What do you mean, 'damned hippie food'?" Rick inquired.

"That organic crap is all natural, and they grow it without fertilizer and stuff, like them damned hippies. Them damned hippies live in the woods with no electricity, wood heat, no running water, and they use only natural stuff like manure and compost to fertilize their land. Damned hippies."

"Zeke, you just described our great-grandparents," Rick replied.

"Well . . . maybe . . . but them damned nature-lovin' hippies have long hair, they don't bathe but once a week or so, don't shave, women don't wear underwear, they have the grandparents, parents, and kids all living in the same commune, and they sit around and smoke wacky-tobacky from a pipe they pass around. Damned drug-smokin', mushroom-eatin' hippies."

"Now, Zeke, you've just described the Native Americans who were here before we were."

"Oh. Well . . . umm . . . I don't care. I don't want none of that damned hippie food. Just give me something decent, like a salami sandwich, fries, a Diet Coke, and a Twinkie."

The Smalltown Busybody

EVERY LITTLE TOWN has at least one person—often (but not always) a woman—whose mission in life seems to be to monitor and spread the news about the lives of her neighbors. In Smalltown, the most prolific busybody was Joline McManus, who, unfortunately, lived across from our family on Eastern Street.

Mrs. McManus was a bitter, unhappy, old widow whose late husband, George, was killed in what the *Smalltown News* called "a tragic train accident" as he was walking home from work. I was a kid at the time and remember overhearing my dad say it wasn't tragic, it was merciful, and it wasn't an accident. Dad thought Mr. McManus chose to jump in front of the Canadian Pacific freight train over spending another thirty years with the old bag. (Mom and Dad didn't care much for Mrs. McManus.)

Dad called her "Hoover" because she kept track of our family's affairs as if she was J. Edgar Hoover and we were the FBI's public enemy number one. Hoover used the latest technology—the party line—to keep track of us. For those of you born after 1960, the party line is probably not only unfamiliar, but unthinkable. In those days, most families shared a telephone line with two or three neighbors. You'd have to pick up the phone and listen to know if the line was in use or available. If you heard someone talking, you would hang up with enough enthusiasm to let your neighbor know you were waiting to make a call, or, if you were like Hoover, you'd quietly listen in for useful information.

Mom was more polite than Dad. When Mrs. McManus would interrupt his conversations with my uncle D.I., he would say, "Hang up, Joline. I'm not talking to you, I'm talking *about* you." (For some reason, Hoover didn't care much for my father.)

Jim and Tess Wright, my folks, are kind, wonderful people, but they're not perfect. I tell the following story at the risk of sullying their good reputation.

In 1964, while Dad was away visiting my ailing grandmother, Hoover was busy keeping tight surveillance on my mother's "affairs." While eavesdropping on Mom's telephone conversation with a man, she overheard the following conversation.

"Jim's out of town 'til Thursday, and the kids are in school all day tomorrow. Can you come over tomorrow for lunch and maybe a little . . . umm . . . dessert, if you know what I mean?"

The man on the other end of the line answered, "Of course, Tess. I'd like that . . . a lot. But we can skip the lunch part and go right for the dessert . . . heh-heh."

"Oh, you naughty boy," my mother replied. "I suppose you'll want whipped cream on your dessert?"

"Tess, I think you're the naughty one. I'll see you around noon then?"

"I'll be here . . . and ready. Don't be late."

As it turned out, Mrs. McManus was, as usual, listening in, and was likely more excited than she'd been in anticipation of her own wedding night. At 11:55 a.m. the following day, a 1962 Ford Fairlane pulled into our driveway and Dad emerged from the driver's-side door as my mother rushed to his arms. They embraced and then, in unison, turned to wave at Hoover, whose kitchen curtain moved suddenly in a fruitless attempt to conceal her surveillance.

My parents were in their thirties in 1964. I can't imagine how many times I've heard them recount the story of how they pranked Old Lady McManus, but I can tell they enjoyed their little stunt way more than a good Christian couple should. At times I've wondered how they celebrated Dad's return and their little Hoover hustle. It's hard for me to think that it might have involved the use of whipped dairy products.

Smalltown Sayings

I GUESS THEY CALL THEM colloquialisms. I don't, because that word just doesn't roll off the tongue well. I call them sayings because that's a lot easier to say. Anyway, they are phrases used by the local folk of a particular region to express a thought or opinion.

I'm told by folks who have moved to Smalltown from away that there are some sayings and words that are unique to this area. For instance, I guess other parts of the country have no *dooryard* (the driveway and area near the entrance of a home), or *broadshelf* (countertop), and they go downtown when we go *downstreet*.

I like, and use, many of the sayings I learned growing up in Smalltown. My favorites include:

- *Darker than a pocket:* That's really dark.
- *Higher than a hawk's nest:* Used to complain about something expensive, or to describe the whiskey tenor part of a high lonesome bluegrass song.
- *He needs that like a frog needs sideburns:* He probably doesn't need that.
- *Hungry enough to eat the north end of a southbound skunk:* Famished.
- *It's hot enough to boil an owl:* That'll make you *sweat like a hen haulin' logs.*

- After a blizzard, *the snow is butt-high to a tall cow.*

Many of the sayings make little sense to me. For example:

A bird in the hand is worth two in the bush. Those must have been the words of a man who was inept with a twenty-gauge shotgun. One grouse in the hand isn't enough for a meal. Two in the bush will soon be lunch.

He got the short end of the stick. Huh? Isn't a stick the same length when measured from either end? Oh, now that I think about it, maybe that wasn't the original saying. Maybe the original was: *He got the sh— end of the stick.* That end I can see as something to avoid.

Never look a gift horse in the mouth. First of all, who gives away a horse? Furthermore, where are you supposed to look a gift horse—or any horse, for that matter? In the eyes? That makes sense to me. It would never occur to me to look into a horse's mouth. So why are you telling me not to? Are gift horses prone to gingivitis?

She was dead as a doornail. What *is* a doornail? Do they really make special nails for doors? And, if so, are they really more dead than other nails . . . or screws . . . or bolts . . . ?

My uncle Herbert was very creative with the English language. He really confused me by slaughtering the wording of some local expressions. He'd say things like:

- *I'd have loved to have been a mouse on the wall* for that conversation: Seems like it would have been hard to have gone unnoticed.

- *You scratch your back and I'll scratch mine:* Which is interchangeable with *One back scratches the other,* and caused me to wonder if I was part of a family of contortionists.
- *He was running around like a chicken with his leg cut off:* Sounds like a poultry entree they might serve at IHOP.
- *A stitch in time saves mine:* My what?
- *From the tiny acorn comes the mighty elm:* Really, Uncle Herbert? Oak-kay.

Uncle Herbert once counseled me: "Don't forget, Joey— *a fool and his mother are soon departed,*" to which I replied: "Oh, Uncle Herbert, I'm sorry you and Grammy have to leave so soon."

Part II: Getting Older Ain't for Sissies

The Golden Years

As I've mentioned, growing up in Smalltown, I had a paper route. I delivered the *Smalltown News* on foot, or rode my old Schwinn bicycle. I was some proud of that bike; it was like a two-wheeled Cadillac with chrome fenders, built-in headlights, and rear fender baskets to hold my newspapers and baseball glove.

A lot of my customers were old. Actually, at that time, I thought everyone over thirty was old, but I'm referring to the senior citizens I'd see daily. Now that I've been offered membership to AARP, my idea of old is changing. Sixty is the new forty, right?

I know "The Golden Years" aren't all they're cracked up to be some days, but for those lucky enough to reach sixty-five or so in fairly good health, I can see some real perks.

First of all, there's retirement. At thirty, I think most of us dream of a career that ends at age fifty. At fifty, reality sets in and we hope for retirement at sixty. At sixty, the idea of a "fixed income" scares the bejeebers out of us, and we resign ourselves to a few more years with our nose to the grindstone.

I get a kick out of retirees who feel they need, or deserve, a discount on everything from a cup of coffee to a Caribbean cruise because they are on a "fixed income." Heck, I don't know about the rest of you working-class stiffs, but after three years of recession, I'd kill for a fixed income. Besides, don't Social Security recipients get a cost-of-living increase every year?

Have you noticed that all those geriatric folks, with nothing to do all day, are always in a hurry? They hate to wait for anything, and expect front-of-the-line privileges in every restaurant, movie theater, and doctor's office. What is it they are in such a rush to get home to—Dr. Phil? Please . . . I'd rather be standing ten deep in line at Dan's Market while holding feminine hygiene products for the little woman.

The other great advantage to aging, as I see it, is that the rules of the road seem not to apply to drivers over seventy. There's no longer any need to acknowledge yield signs or traffic lights. Senior citizens have the right-of-way in all traffic situations—so much so that there's no longer any need to look when backing up the vehicle or approaching an intersection. Just hit the accelerator and go for it. The young people need to be paying attention.

I'm also looking forward (and it's not so far forward anymore) to the day when I decide there's no longer any reason to worry about my appearance. It seems that, for most folks, there comes a day when you wake up and say, "I'm tired of riding the fashion train and I'm jumping off, right now." Sometimes when the little woman, Winnie, and I sneak into the early-bird seating at the chain restaurants, I wonder where all the older guys find those lightweight, light blue, stretch-waist jeans ("dungarees") and white patent-leather shoes. I never see them for sale at Small-Mart, but I sure see a lot of them when I'm scarfing down the $7.99 Ultimate Trio at Applebee's.

For an elderly gentleman, there's another potential perk for reaching your late seventies in good health. My uncle Jack is a confirmed bachelor. Essentially all of his friends took the traditional life path and married in their teens or early twenties. Most of them are dead now. Uncle Jack says it's because after fifty-some years of living with the same woman, they all wanted to die.

Whatever the reason for his buddies' early demise, the consequence is that Uncle Jack, a fairly healthy eighty-year-old with a driver's license, has at his beck and call a veritable harem of widows. Imagine the advantages for a gentleman surrounded by a bevy of gray- and blue-haired ladies, women who were raised to serve their loved ones and can cook from scratch. None of that Lean Cuisine or Hamburger Helper crap for Uncle Jack these days.

All of this newfound attention has gone to my uncle's head. He fancies himself a Smalltown Hugh Hefner. He doesn't lounge around in silk bathrobes, but thinks he's looking good in his yellow turtleneck, madras plaid sport jacket, white belt and shoes, and thirty-year-old, bright green polyester slacks.

After Uncle Jack returned from one of those senior center–sponsored bus trips to Atlantic City, I noticed that his social life seemed to have slowed down a bit. When I asked why he'd been spending so much time alone recently, he told me, "Those old girls are just jealous of my new girlfriend."

It seems my favorite uncle was betting a few chips at the roulette table when a young lady in a tight-fitting red dress and high heels sat down next to him.

"Her name is Ginger, and she took a likin' to me right off," Uncle Jack told me. "And didn't she smell some good—not like lilacs or roses like Gladys and Mildred," he explained. "She told me her perfume was called Passion, and I can tell you, Joey, she is one passionate girl. She was rubbin' up against me like Abbie [his beagle] does when she's lonely, or needs to go out and pee."

I was starting to get the feeling that Ginger was a professional flirter as my uncle continued. "She asked if I'd buy her a cocktail—a Gizmo or a Condo or somethin' like that. All I know is that it was pink and came in a fancy little glass and set me back about thirty clams."

Uncle Jack explained how that drink seemed to send Ginger into a spell of desire for him. "Next thing I know, she's touchin' my leg and whisperin' in my ear—my good ear—how if I'd buy a $500 bottle of champagne, she'd show me her room and a real good time, if ya get my drift." He raised his eyebrows a few times to be sure I understood.

"So what did you do, Unk?" I couldn't wait to hear.

"I told her I don't even like champagne. She gave me her cellular telephone number and told me to call her if I changed my mind. Next thing I know, she was gone like a ghost."

"Did you call her?" I asked.

"Not yet," he replied. "I figure come spring, I'll give her a jingle and ask her up ta camp for a weekend. I'm pretty sure she'd like it up ta Island Lake . . . and God knows, she sure took a shine to me. Probably 'cause I'm a sharp dresser."

I smiled. "Probably," I replied. "But you might want to mend fences with Gladys and Mildred and them, just in case Ginger doesn't like to travel."

"I s'pose you're right, Joey. I ain't had a home-cooked meal in about two weeks."

While there seem to be some advantages to aging, I'm in no rush to get closer to life's finish line. I recognize that I'm a lot closer to the end of my journey. I can see now that this race called life is run on a circular track, and I'm going to end up pretty close to where I started . . . bald, fat, and in diapers.

No More Smokin' Joe

I STARTED SMOKING cigarettes—Lucky Strikes—at fifteen years old. I was in love with sixteen-year-old Rhonda Stevens and wanted to seem older, cooler, and more sophisticated. I was pretty sure a cigarette hanging from my pimple-covered face would drive Rhonda to a state of uncontrollable lust for my bony body.

I just knew that if I smoked, I'd look as cool as James Dean or Cool Hand Luke. (Turns out I actually resembled Joe Camel, the cool Camel cigarette mascot.)

Like James Dean, I wore a tight white T-shirt and stored my Lucky Strikes in the left sleeve. Part of my reason for quitting cigarettes years later was that my shape changed—my belly grew as my biceps withered away—which caused the T-shirt to fit tightly around my gut but loosely at my arm, resulting in the frequent loss of expensive cigarettes.

As a young man, I thought I was ten feet tall and bullet-proof. I'd never look, feel, or grow old. I'd live forever. I'm here to tell you, that hasn't worked out for old Joe. As the years passed, the smokes started to take their toll. I noticed I tired more easily and would experience shortness of breath, especially after extreme exertion, like the time I lost the remote control and had to get off my La-Z-Boy and walk to the TV to change the channel.

Doc Braley warned me I was on a direct path to a heart attack or stroke if I didn't give up the tobacco products. He's such a Gloomy Gus—never sees the sunny side of life.

"You're gonna kill yourself with those cancer sticks, Joe."

Yeah, whatever.

"Plus, you're more likely to develop erectile dysfunction if you smoke," Doc explained.

Yeah, whatever . . . "What? You mean I wouldn't be able to . . ."

"That's right, Joe. You heard me."

Now he had my attention. He'd never told me cigarettes could ruin my life!

I used to buy a pack of smokes for about a Kennedy half-dollar. They were cheap. When they got to be about fifty bucks a carton, that was the last straw.

I did the math one night—with the help of my two-year-old grandson, Hanson, and the calculator app on his iPad—and figured out that comes to about $3,000 per year.

I quit smoking cold turkey right then and there. After all, three grand will buy a lot of Miller Lite.

This Medication Will Help You
(If It Doesn't Kill You)

THE OLDER I GET, the more I worry about my health. Like most young fools at twenty, I thought I'd live forever—always healthy, no wrinkles, no gray hair, and no hair loss. I'd be the first to get out of this world alive, well, and looking good. Thirty-some years later, I'm here to tell you that's not working out so well for me.

I'm happy to say that I am, for the most part, quite healthy. Still, I have more aches and pains than I used to. I never feel 100 percent comfortable anymore. My shoulder will ache for two weeks, and as soon as that feels better, I'll develop a bunion on my little toe. Three weeks of liquid corn-removal therapy and my foot feels fine, but now my teeth hurt, and I find out I need a root canal.

I've noticed that lately it doesn't take much for me to injure myself. Last week, I bent over to pick up a candy wrapper on the sidewalk and threw my back out. Guess I won't lift anything that heavy again.

For a mostly healthy old dude, I've gotten to know a lot of doctors in the past few years. When I was growing up in Smalltown, we had one family doctor and one dentist. Dr. Braley could fix anything from acne to a heart attack. There were no referrals to dermatologists or cardiologists. Dr. B did it all. If he couldn't fix you . . . well, you suffered and then you died. He delivered babies, removed ruptured appendices, performed tonsillectomies, and even did surgeries to prevent young couples from having that seventh or eighth little mouth to feed. (There weren't any magic pills back then.)

The dentist in Smalltown was Dr. Carter. I remember him well. He didn't believe in using novocaine. I'm not sure if he was a sadist or just figured that if he hurt me enough, I'd remember to brush my teeth. At any rate, if you had a dental problem, Dr. Carter would fix it. He'd either drill it and fill it or yank it out.

These days, there seems to be a specialist for every ailment. It takes a separate phone book just to list all the doctors in my little area. There's a special dentist for every part of the mouth. I've seen different dentists to fill cavities, pull teeth, fix my roots, cut my gums, and straighten my smile. There are special doctors for corneas, ankles, hands, feet, prostates, skin, bones, hair loss, weight gain, nerves, tops, bottoms, insides, outsides, front ends, and rear ends. The list could go on for pages.

For all my little aches and pains, I've been lucky so far. I don't have to take any prescription medications. The little woman, Winnie, started taking a blood pressure pill about a month ago, and I haven't had any food with flavor since. She's become a sodium Nazi—"No salt for you!" I think she's perturbed that I eat twice as much and exercise half as much and she's the one with hypertension. Sometimes it's better to be lucky than good.

Since apparently only older geezers watch the evening news, the advertisements are almost exclusively for drugs.

Just as there are doctors for every ailment, there seems to be a drug for every condition. You'd think there was money to be made fixing sick people. Watching these commercials, I don't think I want to take any of these medications. The potential side effects are terrifying! At the end of each commercial there is always someone listing all the bad stuff the drug can do while treating your illness.

"While taking this-costs-a-lot-u-fool, you may experience incontinence, problems with bladder control, or other leakages." Heck, I experience that just listening to the ad. "If you develop bleeding from the eyes, nose, mouth, or ears, become paralyzed, develop loss of memory, vision, hearing, or taste, or have difficulty breathing or swallowing, contact your doctor. These side effects may not be a good thing." Ya think?

"If you are taking an antidoxythyrobenzochorazine inhibitor blocker, you should not take this-costs-a-lot-u-fool." Do you really think I'd know it if I was taking that kind of drug?

One of the blood pressure drugs warned about loss of libido as a side effect. The little woman called my doctor the next morning and asked if he could prescribe that for me. His advice was, "Just say no." Like she hadn't already thought of that.

My blood pressure creeps up from time to time, and I'm sure I'll have to join the millions on drugs eventually. I'm imagining the first follow-up visit with my doctor to see how the this-costs-a-lot-u-fool is working.

Doc: "So, Joe, how are you feeling?"

Me: "Well, Doc, since I've been taking the medication, I vomit every morning, have frequent nosebleeds, can't sleep, have difficulty breathing, and I've developed various leakages."

Doc: "But the medication is working. Your blood pressure is down to 135/75."

Me: "Oh, and Doc, one more thing: I've suddenly developed the urge to commit homicide."

I'm Fat, But It's Not My Fault

I WAS A SKINNY KID during my years at Smalltown High. I was on the track team and ran several miles a day, nearly year-round. I can remember eating fattening stuff, like ice cream and cake, when I wasn't even hungry, just to try to keep my weight up. That's no longer a problem for me.

Like most guys my age, I've bulked up by about fifty pounds since graduating from high school. And it's not like I've pumped iron or taken anaerobic steroids to build muscle mass. I've just gotten fat.

It's not that I like being fat; it's just that I'd rather be fat than hungry. Like my similarly chubby buddy, Barney, likes to say, "I can resist anything but temptation."

I go on a low-calorie diet almost every Monday morning, right after I weigh—and then swear at—myself: "Dammit, Joe, you gotta quit eatin' so much."

My willpower generally lasts until I get to work, and Candi—a hundred pounds of fitness—brings in a fresh-baked batch of raspberry fudge brownies she's never tasted. They smell like they were baked in Heaven, so I try just one, to be polite. I promise myself I'll be good the rest of the day. And I usually am . . . until nighttime. It's Candi's fault I'm fat.

The little woman is a fantastic cook and always has a delicious meal waiting for me after a hard day's labor . . . or even after my typical, put-in-my-time, slacker days. Winnie is equal parts Rachael Ray and Martha Stewart when it comes to food. She's another reason I'm fat. It's certainly not *my* fault.

I'm a fast eater. Put a good meal in front of me and I attack it like a beagle over a bowl of Chicken McNuggets. Gobbling down my dinner seems to make me hungry. After the gnashing of teeth, grunting, moaning, and belching are done, I throw my dirty dishes into the sink and settle onto the sofa for an *Everybody Loves Raymond* marathon.

To make my situation worse, I've followed my father's footsteps and have become a commercial cook. At every commercial, I get up from the couch, waddle to the kitchen, and cook some leftovers.

I like every kind of food—even fruits, salads, and vegetables. But I *really* like chocolate and ice cream. The little woman knows about my weaknesses (and would be happy to provide you with a long, written list), so she rarely picks up sweets at Dan's Market. She knows I want to lose a few pounds and tries to help me in that endeavor. Last summer, she even suggested I go out for a jog in the evenings. That didn't work out so well.

It seems my jogging route happened to coincide with the route of the Mister Softee ice-cream truck. As I've explained, I can resist anything but temptation, and just as I'd run off a quarter of the calories of the Fudgsicle I'd purchased on Eastern Street, he'd stop again . . . and so would I. Mister Softee is to blame for the five pounds I gained jogging last summer.

I've resigned myself to the idea that I'll never lose the twenty pounds I should, so I maintain my self-esteem by watching *The Biggest Loser*, a TV show about people who try to lose 150 pounds so they can be my size; and I spend more time at Small-Mart, where, compared to most of the other shoppers, I'm a little guy.

Eye Anxiety

ABOUT EVERY TWO YEARS or so, I get a postcard from my eye doctor inviting me to go in for another exam. I don't know why, but I think I'd rather have a colonoscopy. It makes me nervous, I guess, to have to answer all those questions: "Which is better, number one or number two?" It's a lot of pressure. What if I answer wrong a couple of times? Will I see upside down and backwards with my new glasses? I'm breaking into a cold sweat just thinking about it.

And what if the doctor gives me bad news? I'd rather die than lose my vision. It just wouldn't be the same having the little woman read *Uncle Hank's Trading Post* to me. Also, what's up with that air-puff test? Does that tell them something about my eyes, or is my doctor just a mean, perverted, sick, little man?

I reluctantly decided to go in for my eye exam last month (actually, Winnie made the appointment and told me I was going). As if I wasn't feeling enough anxiety, I get to the eye-care place to find out that old Dr. A, whom I've seen for twenty-five years, is "out sick." I think "out sick" is doctor-speak for "playing golf."

Anyway, I was told I'd be seeing Dr. B that day. As it works out, Dr. B is a pretty little girl. I guess she must be in her twenties, but she looks about fifteen to me. Do you know how long it's been since I was in a darkened room with a young girl asking me which I like better? Now, I was really nervous.

I decided that I should do what any mature man would do in that situation; I'd mess with her. She put that complicated-looking gizmo in front of me and started asking me all those difficult questions.

"Which is better, Mr. Wright—number one or number two?"

"May I see them again?"

"Number one or number two?"

"Well, number one looks bigger and number two looks crooked."

"Does either look clearer?"

"Oh, maybe number one," I answered.

"Okay, how about number three or number four?" she asked.

"Number two."

"No, Mr. Wright, that's not an option. Number three or number four?"

"Can I see them again?"

(Big sigh.) "Number three or number four?"

"They look the same to me," I replied, chuckling inside.

"Okay, Mr. Wright, try this. Number five or number six?"

"Oh, can I go back to number four? I think that looked a little closer than number three."

"*Aargh!* Never mind, Mr. Wright. I'll just shine this bright light in your eyes and that will tell me your prescription."

"All right, now we're talking!"

Later, I felt a little bad about goofing on that nice little girl doctor. Especially after my eyes stayed dilated for eight, long, bright sunshiny days. Guess Dr. B had the last laugh!

It's Like Pulling Teeth

I LIKE MY DENTIST, Dr. Harding; he's a great guy. I just don't like visiting him at his office. It seems to take him a while to warm up to me. He hardly speaks a word until he and his assistant have four hands, a tongue depressor, that suction thing that seems to get stuck to that soft flesh under my tongue, a mirror, and that high-pitched drill in my mouth. Then he starts asking me questions.

"So Joe, how's Winnie?"

"Aaaahn," I reply. It's the only sound I can make.

"Are you going south this winter?"

"Aah oh eeh oh." That's *I don't think so* with a mouthful of fingers and metal objects.

"Oh, that's too bad. Ann and I are going to Hawaii for three weeks."

"Aaat's ice." That's *Yeah, I think the little woman and I paid for that trip*, with a novocained mouthful.

Actually, I'm more frightened of Dr. Harding's hygienist, Jessica, than I am of him. First of all, it concerns me a bit that she covers me in a lead apron and then leaves the room whenever she takes X-rays of my teeth. I want to say, "Hey, Jessica—if you're afraid to stay in this room with all this radiation, I'm coming out there with you." The problem is, I'm trapped under all that lead and can't get out of the chair.

Jessica probes, prods, and scrapes my teeth for forty minutes and then tells me how clean I'm keeping my teeth. I don't
dare to brush or floss less for fear she'll go in there with a little
sandblaster and jackhammer next time.

When I was a kid, Dr. Carter took care of all my dental
problems . . . *without novocaine.* I think inflicting pain was his
way of promoting dental hygiene. It worked fairly well. After
each painful session with Doc Carter, I'd brush like crazy for
about two weeks. The problem was, I was a kid with a short
attention span and soft teeth. To make things worse, floss
hadn't been invented yet.

Anyway, Doc Carter filled my cavities, pulled teeth, treated
abscesses, and took care of essentially anything else I needed
in the way of dental care. Now I see Dr. Harding, an oral
surgeon, a "gum guy," a lady who does my root canals, and
an endodontist for my $5,000 implant. It hurts me to add up
what I've spent on my teeth in the past five years.

It just occurred to me that my favorite foods are mashed
potatoes, ice cream, pudding, and Cool Whip. If I had to do
it all again, I think I'd invest in a trip to Maui with the little
woman, a brand-new pickup with all the bells and whistles . . .
and dentures.

My High School Reunion

I'M AN ALUMNUS of Smalltown High School, home of the
Smalltown Balmers. You see, Smalltown isn't famous for much,
but it is the home of Bag Balm, the amazing treatment for
cracked udders and hands. Our mascot is a Holstein heifer.

I recently attended the Smalltown High School Class of
1970 reunion. Okay, Einstein, you're right, that's more than
forty years. I can't believe it either! I remember attending my
fifth class reunion and seeing the members of the class of 1935
and wondering how those old folks could even get around.
I felt bad for those decrepit geezers; I was sure their days on
Earth were numbered. Now, I am one of them.

Smalltown High has a well-organized alumni association
because the school is an important part of the community.
Let's face it: There isn't much else here, which is not such a
bad thing. Most of us graduated and never moved away. Why
would anyone leave a town like this? We've got all we need.
There's Dan's Market, Luigi's Lounge, the New Moon Drive-
In Theater (an important part of our culture, since so many
Smalltown residents started their families there), and now
there's Small-Mart, just twenty miles away in Cowville.

Anyway, the Smalltown High School Alumni Association
holds an alumni weekend each June during which each class
celebrating a five-year-interval anniversary gets together.
There are individual class events as well as group activities,

including the Cow Flop Raffle and the Miss Bag Balm Pageant (the winner is a Holstein heifer with exceptional teats).

At my recent reunion, I saw the classes of 2005, 2000, 1995, etc., and it reminded me of some of the Class of 1970 reunions I've attended. In 1975, at our five-year reunion, we were all just as stupid and immature as we were in 1970. Most of us were still more interested in drinking beer and driving fast cars than anything else. Rick Carlson, our quarterback, came and impressed us all with his stories of frat parties and his college football prowess. If he'd gone to school with more than five hundred students, I'm sure he'd have been a Heisman candidate. Lisa Sampson, the prettiest girl in our class, was still single and as "hot" as in 1970 . . . and she was still out of my league.

Things were different at our tenth reunion. Most of us locals had been married at least once since graduating, and had a couple of kids. We shared photos of our rug rats instead of comparing pictures of Mustangs and Camaros. Rick showed up with a Corvette, an Armani suit, and, I'm guessing, a boat-load of debt. Lisa hadn't eaten for three months and looked like she'd spent most of that time under a sun lamp. My buddy Munzie, who's never had an unspoken thought, told her she looked like a Bangladeshi refugee.

By 1990, some of us had kids who'd graduated from Small-town High School. There were even a few grandparents in our class. I, of course, was much too young for that. Rick Carlson didn't show up that year; Munzie heard he'd lost his 'Vette, his house, and a lot of cash to a very wealthy ex-wife. Lisa was on her third husband and still pretty . . . pretty close to 250 pounds. She was still tanned, too. Her skin was the texture of fine Corinthian leather. Barney Prince said she looked good from afar and far from good.

I must say it was nice to see some of my old friends at our recent reunion. We're each at a place in our lives where we feel no need to impress one another. My only disappointment was that a lot of my classmates were thinner than me. I was surprised, because I'm not that fat compared to most guys my age (especially at Small-Mart).

It took me a while to figure out why I had a good twenty-five pounds on most of the guys at our reunion: Most of my fat classmates were smart enough to avoid embarrassment by staying home.

I'm Comfortable in My Old Skin

I DON'T UNDERSTAND. I'm a lot bigger than I used to be, but my skin is too loose for my body. My outer layer wiggles, jiggles, folds, and wrinkles to the point that I could probably remove enough skin to cover a small teenager, and still have enough left over for me. Still, I'm comfortable in this old skin—probably more comfortable than ever before. Maybe it's because it fits like an oversized pair of cotton sweatpants. Or maybe it's just because as I get older, I realize my prospects for a modeling career are pretty much dead. That is, unless some entrepreneur opens a catalog business catering to the ever-increasing number of old, fat guys in this country—J. Crude? The Nap? Old R Us?

I'm afraid I care a lot less about how I appear to the opposite gender these days. After thirty-plus years, the little woman, Winnie, has gotten used to having me around, and I don't think she's likely to kick me to the curb at this point. These days, I'm a lot more excited by her prowess in the kitchen than in the bedroom, and I'm almost certain she'd rather please me with scampi than whoopee. That may sound sad to younger folks, but it's a pretty comfortable place to be.

I've noticed that the more birthdays I have, the less I care about what other people think of me. I pretty much say what I think (sometimes to the horror of my children). So, excuse me for being honest, but my daughter's friend Nicki (the former

Miss Smalltown High Queen) *does* look pregnant; my aunt Becky is a pain in the backside and *does* need a shave; and our waitress last week *does* look too old to be working at Hooters.

Winnie and the kids seem to worry about some of the outfits I wear in public.

"Dad, you can't go to town wearing short-shorts [I guess the style changed a few years ago], a white T-shirt, and black work boots!"

"Why not?" I asked. "I think I look fine."

"You'll embarrass yourself, Dad."

"Nope. I don't care what folks think; I'm comfortable."

"Well, you'll embarrass me."

"All right. I'll change into my 2 SEXY 2 B 40 T-shirt. Hope it still fits around my belly."

I used to worry about stupid stuff. Now I live by the old mantra: "Don't sweat the small stuff—and remember, it's all small stuff."

This past November, I was deer-hunting with my much younger, and therefore more worrisome, brother, K.C., up to our camp just north of Smalltown, when three inches of fresh "tracking snow" fell on Sunday evening.

"I won't be goin' to work tomorrow," I told him.

"Ain't worried about losin' your job, Joe?" he replied.

"Hell, no, I ain't worried." I went on to explain my lack of concern. So what if I got fired? Winnie and I would be fine. We live in the "land of milk and honey." Or is it "milk the system"? This is 2011, and my government will take care of me whether I carry my own weight or not, especially this new president. He'll just reach his magic hand into the bottomless pot of money, pull some out, and send it to me. It's free, and there's an endless supply. I think Keebler elves or leprechauns are working double shifts to make more of it. I don't have to do anything. So what if I can't pay my mortgage? The government will take care of that. They'll give me a nice place to live, free food, and medical care. It's all free, thanks to hard-working worriers like my little brother.

No, I won't lose any sleep over the small stuff. In the words of *Mad* magazine's Alfred E. Neuman: "What, me worry?" I may look like one of those dogs whose wrinkled-up skin is too big for its body, but I'm comfortable in my old skin.

I Thought I Was Losing My Hair

MY HAIRLINE HAS BEEN RECEDING since I was about twenty; that's no surprise. The Wright boys, going back several generations, have developed "male pattern baldness" at an early age. I think it's because we have too much testosterone—the male hormone. We're apparently manlier than guys like Brad Pitt and George Clooney, who go through a lot more shampoo than we do.

I have to admit that, for years, I was bothered by my apparent hair loss. It seemed as though the ladies were attracted to those unmanly men with full heads of hair. Consequently, I tried some of the ways that guys like me attempt to conceal, or remedy, our follicular challenges.

My uncle Herb had no hair on the top of his head. As my buddy Barney would say, "His hairline isn't receding; it's in full retreat." My uncle's solution was the classic comb-over. He'd part his hair just above his left ear and comb it to cover the barren area at the top of his head. He had everyone fooled (really?), and was feeling quite sexy, until he was riding on Barney's outdoor power equipment float at the Smalltown Memorial Day parade in 2007. Uncle Herb's hair spray wasn't adequate to hold his comb-over down in the high winds, but did cause it to move as one unit. He looked like he had a foot-tall sail atop his noggin. When a particularly strong gust blew, it caught Unk's hair sail and knocked him right off a Toro riding mower and onto the street, where he wiped out half the Smalltown High School baton-twirling team.

I've never considered a toupee; I guess I've seen too many bad ones. Maybe I've seen a lot of good ones and don't even know it . . . but I doubt it. Burt Reynolds had a good hairpiece—and a lot of money. Maybe that's why I've seen so many bad rugs; my social circle is not exactly "upper crust." I don't understand why a guy with light brown hair would glue a black toupee to the top of his head.

My uncle Jack was an avid hunter and outdoorsman who went from totally bald to a full head of hair overnight. It seems he took a liking to Polly Prindall, the cashier down at the Smalltown IGA. So, he fashioned a hairpiece out of part of a beaver pelt. They tell me that Polly (and many others) enjoyed a good laugh at my uncle's expense. Uncle Jack didn't get a date with Polly, but his head was warmer that January while cutting holes in the ice to tend his traps.

My brother-in-law Jimbo started losing his hair from the back, forward, a few years ago, and decided to cover the bald spot at the back of his head with some of that spray-on hair. It looked *really* natural; my brother K.C. and I had Jimbo convinced of it. He was going through about a can a week and feeling good about himself (my sister, Vanessa, is too kind to have told him it looked like he had a cow flop on his head), until he got caught in a downpour and the dark brown goop oozed onto, and stained, his favorite LOVE MACHINE T-shirt.

I once considered Rogaine, hair weaves, Hair Club for Men, and special shampoos, but they all seemed like too much trouble or money. I've seen guys who had hair from the back of their head transferred in little implants to the front. Something about that never looks quite right. It's like someone planted a row of corn and forgot to fertilize it. No thank you.

As it turns out, I'm not losing my hair; I've just misplaced it. The thick, wavy locks that once grew from the follicles atop my hat rack now emanate from places I don't need hair. There are elf-like tufts billowing from my ears, seemingly causing me to miss some of the important things Winnie says to me, like, "Honey, could you take the trash out when you get a chance?" Or, "Sweetheart, could you hand me the remote? I'm tired of watching *The Bassmaster Marathon.*"

I own a nose-hair trimmer now; that's a lot of fun to use. It's like a mini weed-whacker for the nostrils. I've grown enough hair on my back in the past few years to look like I've only recently evolved from my Cro-Magnon ancestors. The weirdest development, though, is that from time to time, the little woman will find a four-inch-long, thin white hair growing from the middle of my forehead. It seems to show up overnight as one of Mother Nature's cruel jokes.

I keep waiting for a miracle pill that will restore my hair to its former glory. In the meantime, I'll continue to alternate between the blue ball cap with the big red "B" and the Patriots hat, which looks a lot like Elvis.

I Wonder What My Gravestone Will Say

I TOOK A WALK WITH MY BEAGLE BOOZER recently, and we ended up in the Smalltown cemetery. I noticed there were headstones dating back to the early nineteenth century, and I read many of the inscriptions. As I did so, it occurred to me that most of the gravestones said little about the person buried there, other than the length of his or her life.

I want my gravestone to be different. The mark I leave on this world may be smaller than a gnat's eye, but I want anyone reading my headstone to know something about me.

There are some inscriptions I *don't* want on my stone. A couple of them come to mind:

> JOE WRIGHT
> HE WORKED TOO MUCH
> AND PLAYED TOO LITTLE

or,

> JOE WRIGHT
> HE DIDN'T HAVE MUCH FUN
> BUT HE HAD A LOT OF MONEY

or,

> JOE WRIGHT
> 1952 TO (ANYTHING LESS THAN 2032)

or,

> JOE WRIGHT
> SADLY MISSED BY ALMOST NO ONE

I do have some ideas for inscriptions that I would find acceptable for my gravestone. For instance:

JOE WRIGHT

DEVOTED HUSBAND AND FATHER

FAN OF THE RED SOX, THE PATS, AND PBR

Or maybe an inscription that tells the story of my demise would let visitors to my grave know that I enjoyed life right to the end:

JOE WRIGHT

1952–2042

LOVING HUSBAND OF WINNIE WRIGHT (1957–2040)

KILLED IN BED BY A JEALOUS YOUNG HUSBAND

(DO THE MATH)

In the end, we're all here for a very short while, and we leave little behind except a few loved ones and a few words chiseled in stone. Maybe I'll be lucky and my final resting place will be adorned by a beautiful chunk of granite, into which the following words will be etched:

JOE WRIGHT

1952–2040

DEVOTED HUSBAND AND FATHER

PATRIOT AND OUTDOORSMAN

DIED AT 88 OF A HEART ATTACK SUSTAINED WHILE DRAGGING OUT

A STATE RECORD 12-POINT WHITETAIL BUCK

RIP

The Evening News

I GUESS I'M A CREATURE OF HABIT. I still watch the evening
news on television every night, though it rarely leaves me feeling warm and fuzzy. I'm not sure why I feel compelled to tune
in to find out that my 401(k) plan is shrinking faster than this
year's *Biggest Loser,* or that the national debt is growing at the
same rate as Oprah, or that the CEO of some corporation that
we taxpayers have recently bailed out just received a bonus
equal to the annual payroll of the New York Freakin' Yankees
. . . but I do. It's been a part of my daily routine since November 22, 1963. (Damn you, Lee Harvey Oswald!)

I grew up watching Walter Cronkite, and I liked him. He
was like a grandfather to me, and had a great voice. Besides,
he was on the one channel we could pick up on our roof
antenna long before cable came to Smalltown.

Later on, I got my daily dose of reality TV from Dan Rather
or Tom Brokaw, and they were okay, too, but I miss Charlie
Gibson the most. Charlie (I feel like we're on a first-name
basis) just seems like a regular guy . . . an Average Joe. He has
fairly plain features and slightly crooked teeth, and he talked
to me like he was my next-door neighbor—the one I like, *not*
the one who complains about every little thing (like my loud
banjo music, my errant golf ball breaking his bay window, or
that grass fire that got away from me and burned an acre or so
of his lawn the weekend before his daughter's outdoor, home

wedding). Anyway, I didn't mind all the bad news as much when it came from my friend Charlie.

I'm not sure which is more disturbing—the news, or the advertising that runs during the evening news broadcast. I get chest pains just watching all the commercials telling me about the high incidence of heart disease and hypertension among folks my age. And all these ads about diabetes testing supplies upset me so much, I go to the kitchen and cook myself a snack every time a commercial comes on.

I know I'm not the only one annoyed by all those erectile dysfunction remedies. Every time one of these ads shows a romantic scene featuring a couple of sexagenarians, I give the little woman my sexy look, to which she always replies, "Don't bother." I guess I won't risk the potential stroke, blindness, rejection, or that "problem" lasting more than four hours. It would probably just bring back bad memories of getting all suited up in my football uniform just to spend the entire game on the bench.

I wish more young people would watch Scott Pelley, Brian Williams, or Diane Sawyer. Maybe there would be more ads about sexy cars, flame-broiled Whoppers, cold Bud Light, or Victoria's Secret.

Some Old Guys Give Me Hope

I LIKE TO HAVE BREAKFAST down at the Miss Smalltown Diner. The food there is nothing to rave about, which may explain their "no wait—no hurry" attitude. I go to the diner because of the other people I see there, especially the old guys—really old guys—that give me hope that there can be good quality of life after the age of seventy.

There's a booth in the corner near the Wurlitzer that's unofficially reserved for three old guys every Monday through Saturday. Rene Gagne, Herve Ouellette, and Conrad Frechette show up each morning at about six-thirty and nurse a coffee and toast until around eight, at which time they get on with their busy lives. Rene, Herve, and Conrad have a lot in common. They are all over ninety, of French-Canadian descent, have outlived their wives, believe in hard work, and like pretty women.

Rene worked for the Canadian Pacific Railroad for forty-five years laying track, as well as utilizing his sandblasting and welding skills to refurbish freight and passenger cars. I always try to sit at a booth or counter stool adjacent to the old guys so that I can overhear their colorful conversations.

Last Tuesday, Rene, at ninety-two years old, was upset because of the weather forecast. "Dat weather girl on WMTW, you know, dat short, fat one, said mostly sunny today, so yesterday I pull all the shingles off the top of my roof. Now it rains and dat roof leaks like a son-of-a-biscuit. Dat chubby weather girl should come over and help me cover my furniture, but she's probably too busy eatin' dem damn jelly donuts."

Herve, at ninety-three, is a rugged, stocky, loud Frenchman with a boisterous laugh and a wonderful sense of humor. He lost his wife in 1967, and then his longtime girlfriend, Yvette, about a year ago. "I go out to split a half cord of maple, and when I come in for my Old Milwaukee, there she is, dead as a doorknob, watching *All My Children*," he told Conrad. "I miss Yvette and I want to find another girlfriend, but not a ninety-year-old—they don't last. I need me a young one; between seventy-five and eighty would be good."

Conrad Frechette is a bit younger; he just celebrated his ninetieth birthday at the retirement home where his little girl, Jeanette, lives. (She turned seventy-one last August.) Conrad likes to stay busy and is a dapper old guy. He wears a plaid flannel shirt with a tie every day, and works hard to stay in good physical condition. He does an hour in his basement with free weights and a stationary bike every morning. He delivers meals to elderly shut-ins four days a week. "Dem old people needs my help," he says. "Dey need good food, too, don't you know.

"Besides dat," he continues, "some dem girls are pretty cute, and dey like ol' Conrad 'cause I stay in good shape. Ol' Conrad gets a lot of cupcakes . . . if you know what I means."

I hear a lot of octogenarians complain about "The Golden Years." There's no doubt that getting old ain't for sissies, and it makes me wonder if I want to go down that road. Guys like Herve, Conrad, and Rene give me hope that if I take care of myself and maintain a positive attitude, ninety-something might not be so bad.

Besides, I like cupcakes.

Part III: The Great Outdoors

Hunting Camp Characters

I'VE BEEN GOING TO DEER CAMP for well over forty years—to the Wright Boys Camp up near Island Lake every year—but also to several others, at times, through my life. I've noticed that all camps have some characters in common.

There's always The Loudmouth—the guy who just never shuts up, and spends most of his time blabbering on about his favorite subject . . . himself. Some of the guys I hunt with would be very content to stay in camp all day, consume adult beverages, eat chili, pass gas, and play cards; but they'd rather go out at minus-twenty degrees Fahrenheit and develop piles from sitting on a frozen rock for six hours than stay in and endure the ramblings of The Loudmouth.

And, there's always The Storyteller. He tells the same stories several times every deer season, but he's not totally repetitious because he lies, and consequently, can't remember how he's told the tall tales in the past. So far, he's shot the same twelve-pointer with his shotgun, his .30-06, and his .303 Savage. That deer weighed 202 to 246 pounds, depending on how many Wild Turkeys preceded the story. Sometimes, he dragged that big buck four miles—all uphill—back to camp. Other nights he wounded the animal, which ran back two miles toward his truck, and was kind enough to drop dead ten yards away from his tailgate.

There seems to be The Moocher in every camp, too—the guy who shows up with no food, a six-pack of beer (two hours' worth), just enough cash for poker, and a huge appetite. He always offers an excuse and a promise, but little else.

"I was going to bring up a big pot of moose-meat stew, but the old lady didn't make it in time. I'll bring it next weekend, for sure." He's the same guy who never cooks a meal or washes a dish. He gets invited back every year only because he's a relative and you can't choose them.

Every camp has The Bragger, too. Up to the Wright Boys Camp, there's a guy who, unfortunately, shot the biggest buck ever taken out of that cabin. He fell asleep in his tree stand and, when he regained consciousness, the monstrous animal (temporarily stupid because of his total obsession with does in heat), was lying down forty yards in front of him, apparently resting between lovemaking forays. That buck was the only deer The Bragger ever shot, but we've heard about it over and over for thirty years now.

So, there's The Loudmouth, The Storyteller, The Moocher, and The Bragger. But enough about me. There are those other characters, too.

The Joker knows hundreds of funny stories and can recall them at the mention of a word in a punch line. Everyone in camp has heard all of his jokes at least a hundred times, but we laugh with every repeat performance because The Joker is really good at acting out the stories, and speaks with foreign accents and speech impediments. For some reason, he's always funniest on Jose Cuervo Night at deer camp.

Seems like every camp I visit has The Sleeper. My cousin
Smitty is The Sleeper at the Wright Boys Camp. He naps in
the recliner in front of the woodstove for at least six hours
a day, goes to bed right after dinner (but before clean-up or
wood-splitting), and wakes up tired at ten a.m., just in time for
his one-hour hunt. I don't know what Old Sleepy does when
he's not up at camp. I figure he must stay awake from Labor
Day until deer season, and then catches up on his shut-eye.

There's The Slob in every camp, too. You can track him
like a deer by following the trail of empty beer cans, coffee
cups, and dishes he leaves scattered throughout the cabin. As
you might expect, his personal hygiene isn't all it could be,
either. He does fairly well at shooting deer and bear. I think
it's because he smells kind of wild, and they mistake him for
one of their own.

A lot of camps have The Home Run King—the guy who
can't wait to get to camp and away from it all, but seems to
come up with a thousand reasons to Run Home. I'm not sure
if he's afraid his little woman misses him, or fears she's not
lonely at all. I'm in luck that way; Winnie seems to enjoy my
absence . . . .

I Don't Mind Roughing It

As MY FATHER LIKES TO SAY, "I don't mind roughing it, as long as everything goes *real smooth.*" Mind you, that's a relatively new philosophy for Dad. When I was a kid, hunting camp had gaslights and an outhouse. These days, my father complains because the light in the microwave doesn't work, and the satellite dish picks up only 105 channels. It's almost enough to make him venture out into the woods to hunt . . . almost.

Lately, the little woman's idea of roughing it is staying in a Holiday Inn instead of a Hilton. I don't mind camping occasionally, though over the years our idea of camping has changed significantly. When the kids were still rug rats, we had two small tents, a cooler, and a Hibachi stove that actually burned charcoal briquettes. Jake and Maggie have fond memories of their dad throwing a match onto the lighter fluid and burning off his mustache, both eyebrows, and those awesome, long, wide sideburns.

Eventually, we graduated to a pop-up, which required a bigger vehicle to pull it around. That did little more than get us up off the ground. Two years later, we moved up to a seventeen-foot trailer with some creature comforts like beds and a propane cookstove. Guess what; I needed an SUV to haul it. Do you see the pattern here?

It wasn't long before we (Winnie) decided we needed a bigger trailer with a shower, toilet, fridge, and stereo system—our aluminum love shack. And, oh yeah, an F-150 pickup to tow it.

I was feeling like we'd gotten away from roughing it until a recent stay at the White Mountains RV Park and Resort. We'd seen giant motor homes in our area before, often parked beside a little house in dire need of paint and a new roof, with three broken-down snowmobiles, two ATVs, and the rusted skeletons of various cars and trucks in the dooryard. But I'd never seen anything you could drive on the road like the "camper" of Thomas R. Howell IV, our weekend neighbor at the RV Resort.

Thomas ("Don't call me Tom") was proud of his gigantic mansion on wheels. That thing seemed to be 120 feet long! He was kind enough to give me the grand tour, and I couldn't believe my eyes. There was a dish antenna on the roof to provide TV and Internet reception. He had automatic levelers and steps, an eighty-inch plasma TV inside, a smaller seventy-inch built into the outside, backup monitors, marble countertops, a full-size refrigerator and cooking appliances, and a live-in cook/maid. In the bath, there was a shower, Jacuzzi hot tub, and something called a bidet, which looked as though if you pushed the button to activate it, it would cause you to emit a high-pitched *Woo-hoo*.

During the course of our weekend "in the wild," I observed Thomas constantly negotiating deals, texting on two Black-Berries while talking nonstop into the Bluetooth hooked to his ear, and e-mailing on either the computer built into his dashboard or the laptop he used from under his fifty-foot awning.

One evening, I was out flipping burgers on my rusty old gas grill as his maid served Thomas and Mrs. Howell coq au vin and Chardonnay.

"It was a nice day, huh?" I offered.

"Marvelous," Thomas replied. "It's great to get away from it all and commune with nature."

The Thirty-Fifth Annual Smalltown Boys Ice-Fishing Extravaganza

PEOPLE WHO COMPLAIN THAT BASEBALL is a slow-moving, boring sport have never been ice-fishing. I've just returned from the Thirty-Fifth Annual Smalltown Boys Ice-Fishing / Beer-Drinking / Fish Tale–Embellishing Extravaganza, and I'm suffering from severe sensory deprivation.

It's the same every year. A dozen or more guys show up at various times on a Friday in February and are segregated into two sporting camps—the old guys' camp and the young bucks' camp. The location for the past ten years or so has been the All Seasons Camps on Big Lake, up north.

I've been attending the annual ritual for twenty years, so I missed the early trips, yet I feel as though I was there because I've heard the stories for two decades. According to legend, in the old days when my fellow old guys were the original young bucks, they roughed it. It was 60 degrees below zero and they took dogsleds onto Lambert Lake. They stayed in igloos with only the heat of the dogs to keep them warm, and they drank heavily from sunup Friday to sundown Sunday. They caught too many ten-pound brook trout to keep. Anything under five pounds was thrown back.

I don't doubt the integrity of my fellow geezers, but I've noticed that over the years, the temperature at Lambert Lake has dropped 30 degrees and the average fish taken has gained several pounds.

Friday night at the annual Ice-Fishing / Beer-Drinking / Fish Tale–Embellishing Extravaganza is the social highlight of the weekend. Guys are happy to see each other again, and celebrate by enjoying an abundance of "wobbly pops." My buddy Barney usually has to mooch a few beers off me to get him through the first night because . . . well . . . they don't make anything bigger than a thirty-pack.

The old guys spend the first evening telling stories and repeating old jokes, slurring punch lines, and laughing as if we hadn't heard them all thirty (or more) times. Being serious fishermen, we're typically in bed by one a.m., doors locked to prevent intrusions by our intoxicated offspring.

The young bucks don't know enough to give up the party before three a.m. They just haven't suffered the ensuing headache and nausea often enough to know better. For the most part, their memory of the night's events ends around midnight, but the beer drinking, food-fighting, table dancing, no-rules card-playing party goes on. Invariably, someone loses consciousness and becomes the subject of a photo-documented dress-up session. He ends up wearing an apron, a wig, lipstick, and a fur hat, and often has a stuffed duck sitting on his head as he unwittingly poses on the sofa for a digital photo shoot—soon to be shared with millions, including his proud, young wife, on the World Wide Web.

Saturday is a different story. These avid, young ice fishermen are up at the crack of ten a.m., looking a bit green, feeling very tired, and wondering what happened. They are noticeably more quiet than on Friday night, obviously totally focused on the fishing.

Our resident guides, Bert and Dave, have spoken to our hosts, Rob and his teenage son, Robbie, and have us hooked up with the ideal fishing spot. Big Lake is six miles long so, needless to say, our "hot spot" is five miles from our camps. But our guides are confident in the insider information they've received from our hosts. These guys live on Big Lake and obviously know where the good fishing is (and keep it to themselves), because their walls and website are covered with trophy pike, bass, trout, and salmon. By the end of the weekend, however, it's becoming obvious they make their living by reeling in two hundred–pound suckers.

This year, the annual ice-fishing trip fell during the Vancouver Winter Olympics, so we decided to award medals for the three longest fish. The sorry truth is that I caught the smallest fish of the day, a twelve-inch white perch, and won the silver medal. Dave's son Todd was the champion, with a whopper thirteen-and-a-half-inch smallmouth bass, and was so proud of his gold medal that he took it home and had it bronzed. You don't have to be the head stock boy at the Smalltown IGA to go ice-fishing.

So, to summarize, on a cold weekend in February, thirteen men converged on Big Lake, ate too much, drank far too many brewskis, woke up Saturday morning with big heads, drove five miles on ATVs to get to the "sweet spot," fished sixty-five tip-ups for seven hours while standing in twenty-five-mile-per-hour winds, and caught two fish, barely bigger than our bait.

I was ready to say *Never again!* until I got home on Sunday and spent six hours watching man-bashing movies on Lifetime with the little woman, after which I promptly e-mailed Bert and Dave to make my reservations for next year's ice-fishing extravaganza.

If Deer Could Talk

EVERY NOVEMBER, I spend a lot of time with other guys dressed in wool and blaze-orange. We spend hours talking about how well we know deer, their feeding and breeding habits, and how they think.

I'd love to be a tick on a deer's back and listen to a conversation between two bucks. Maybe it would go something like this:

"Hey, Wilbur."

"Yeah, Larry."

"It feels like it could snow any day now. I love this time of year."

"Yup. Soon the yahoos will be out in the woods with us again."

"Can't wait."

"So, Wilbur, I don't get it. Every year, they plant those big, round, tasty, orange-colored things and we eat most of them. Then they carve faces into some of them and put them in front of the places where they bed down."

"Yup, Larry, that's how I know it's almost time. Soon they'll dress up like those big, orange-colored, tasty things and come out to the woods."

"Oh cool, Wilbur, here comes one now. He's walkin' this way."

"So why do they walk around on their hind legs?"

"I dunno, Wilbur. No wonder they fall down a lot. And they wonder why they can't keep up with us."

"He's gettin' close, Larry. This'll be fun. Wait for it. Wait for it. Sixty yards . . . fifty yards . . . He stopped. He put that noisy stick over his shoulder. Okay, run!"

Sixty yards later . . .

"Okay. Stop, Larry." (Chuckles.) "Look at him. He's hittin' himself on the head."

"Wilbur, he's walkin' this way. Should we run again?"

"Heck no! Let's sneak around him so we can watch him. He'll do somethin' stupid again. I'm sure of it."

"Here we go. He's puttin' that thing in his mouth and makin' gruntin' noises. What the hay?"

"Larry, I think he's tryin' to talk to us, but he doesn't know our language."

"What's he sayin', Wilbur?"

(Laughter.) "I think he just said, 'I'm a smaller buck than you, and I want you to make love to me.' "

"That's kinda twisted."

"Yeah, Larry, they're a weird breed."

"Lordy, Wilbur, did he just do what I think he did?"

"Yup. Oh God, I can't stop laughin'. He just picked up some of your poop and sniffed it. This is too funny. By the way, Larry, if you ever come across any of their droppin's, don't sniff. I don't know what they eat, but it ain't cedar or acorns, that's for sure."

One hour later.

"Geez, Wilbur, we've been followin' him for a while. What's he doin'?"

"He's hangin' somethin' from a tree. He's takin' somethin' from his fur and squirtin' it. Oh God, Larry, hold your breath. Whoa!"

"Geez, Wilbur, what's that smell?"

"I'm not sure, but I think he's tryin' to smell like a hot doe."

"A hot doe? It'd take a doe ten times the size of big Effie to smell like that. Heck, even Effie's too fat for me, and you know I ain't that fussy."

"That's for sure."

"Wilbur, let's get outta here."

"Not yet, Larry. He's climbin' a tree now. Let's wait. Wait for it. Okay, when he's halfway up the tree, make that snortin' noise and run right past him. His noisy stick is still on the ground. Oh, and Larry, make sure he sees those big bones stickin' out of our heads. That really makes those yahoos do stupid stuff."

Poachers Ain't Hunters

I HATE GAME POACHERS. You know the kind of guy I'm referring to. He's that poor excuse for a human who thinks he's
a hunter because he shoots a lot of deer and moose from his
pickup truck while shining a billion-candlepower spotlight on
them, and then leaves them in some farmer's field to die and
rot. He brags about the deer he shoots legally, but everyone
knows he's lying through his tooth. He's not a man, and he's
certainly not a hunter.

He's the kind of guy who is able to hunt at midnight
because, during the day, he naps. His shiny new F-150 with
the fancy spotlights is parked in the dooryard of his shack
down by the river while his wife works a double shift down at
Dan's Market and his poor, rag-wearing kids are off at school.

I wish there was an open season on deer jackers. Have the
game wardens turn them loose in a field and allow law-abiding
sportsmen to cull the human herd of some of the weak-
minded, amoral, spineless losers that steal the wildlife that
wardens and honest outdoorsmen, like me, seek to preserve
and protect. I'd pay good money for that license permit.

Since I loathe poachers, I like game wardens . . . most game
wardens, that is.

When I was a young man—a long time ago—the warden responsible for the area from Smalltown to Island Lake
was Dain Eldridge. He was a pea-brained, power-hungry,

mean-spirited, arrogant putz. I mean that in the kindest way, of course.

Dain wasn't smart enough to outwit the deer poachers, so he abused the power of his position and wasted taxpayers' dollars by prosecuting dangerous culprits like my grandfather. It seems Gramps had taken my twelve-year-old nephew, Josh, fishing for the afternoon. Josh was visiting for the day from Connecticut, and had no fishing license. Dain nailed Gramps for fishing with two poles, in a pond that was home to nothing but three gazillion yellow perch. My grandfather lost his fishing license for two years, and the world was a safer place, thanks to Dain Eldridge.

Shortly after the little woman and I were married, I was hunting squirrels up near Hogback Knob with my brothers, Sam and K.C., when I found a broken robin's egg on the ground. It was the prettiest shade of blue I'd ever seen. I guess you'd call it . . . well . . . robin's egg blue. I knew Winnie would like it, so I tucked it gently into the little plastic baggie I use to keep my hunting license dry.

Wouldn't you know it? When we returned to my truck, Dain Eldridge was parked there waiting for us. He knew my Dodge Ram, and also knew my brothers and I come from a long line of dangerous perch poachers, so he was likely concerned that we'd get more than our share of the two billion gray squirrels up on Hogback Knob.

Needless to say, when I pulled the baggie from my pocket to show my license, Dain, being blessed with ultra-keen senses, spotted the little blue eggshell.

"Looks like you found a robin's egg," he stated.

"Yup."

"You can't remove that from the woods. It upsets the balance of nature."

That's when I lost it.

"The balance of nature? I can't believe you're preaching to me about the balance of nature! You cleared two acres of beeches and ash trees from what was once the best hunting area in the county so you could put your house and your mother's trailer there, and you have the audacity to chastise me for removing a broken eggshell from the forest? You pea-brained, useless, rubber-spined drain on society. Don't you have something better to do? Why are you bothering me over this used robin's egg?"

"Because I can." Dain smirked. "It's my job."

So now you're sitting there reading about Dain Eldridge, the dim-witted, self-important, spineless, poor excuse for a human being. And do you know why I'm telling this story to millions (okay, maybe hundreds) of readers?

Because I can. It's my job.

Golf . . . A Good Walk Spoiled

GOLF IS A GOOD WALK SPOILED. Mark Twain said it years ago, and there have been many days when I finished up on the links, pulled the calculator out of my golf bag to add up my score, and had to agree with him.

Living here in the North Country, I have all winter to read *Golf Digest,* watch the professionals on TV, and reflect on my game. And, every winter I have my golf swing figured out in my head—*Gentle grip, take the club back slowly, weight over my right foot, cock wrists 90 degrees, smooth forward motion, weight over left foot at impact.* . . . By April, I can't wait to try out my new technique and watch my score plummet. It never works out that way. It takes about two strokes to figure out my game is just as pathetic in April as it was back in October.

Golf course designers are mean people . . . sadists. They take a gorgeous landscape, plant flowers and beautiful trees that blossom, and manicure the grass to lull the average golfer into a state of near euphoria. Then, they use their sick, little, twisted, evil minds to place ponds and creeks and sand traps in the locations most likely to attract my golf ball. (Whichever scientist decided that the top of an oak tree is 90 percent air never hit a golf ball.)

If you've watched the professionals play golf on television, but have never played yourself, I'm sure the game looks easy. I know what you're thinking: *How hard can it be to hit a little ball, sitting perfectly still on a tee, with a big stick? It's not like someone's throw-ing it at you at 100 miles per hour.* The answer: extremely hard! Golf balls like the high grass, woods, water, and sand. I think they are specially designed to be attracted to hazards.

Golf is good for physical fitness, building character, teach-ing one to overcome adversity, and helping to keep a person humble. It is *not* good for a marriage.

Three years ago, the little woman decided to take up golf . . . and I encouraged her. That was dumbness on my part. At first, I couldn't help but offer advice on improving her swing. "Sweetie, keep your eye on the ball. You might want to bend your knees a little more. Your feet were aiming in the wrong direction."

My pointers were neither helpful nor appreciated: "I've seen you play—you should just work on your own pathetic swing" were her exact words.

There are two other problems that have arisen from Win-nie's interest in golf. I hardly ever get a day off to play with just my buddies. Not only do I miss the off-color stories and manly banter, but now Roy, Ted, and Munzie have frequent opportunities to point out that the little woman has out-driven me or has scored a par on the hole I just double-bogeyed. I must say, though, they're not totally insensitive to how I feel. They compliment me sometimes on how far I can throw my putter after missing a three-footer.

It has been reported that Confucius say, "Man who play golf . . . he putz." Average Joe Putz says, "Man who pays for little woman's golf cart . . . he better off buying her a Caddy (a Coupe de Ville, or an Escalade)."

Uncle Herbert Knew How to Catch Trout

I LIKE FISHING FOR TROUT . . . especially brook trout. Putt-putting around a lake or pond at trolling speed is fun and can be relaxing, but I'm easily bored; I've always had a short attention span. I guess that's why I prefer to pull on the hip boots and work my way down a fast-moving stream. I'm also partial to using worms for bait. Some purists feel like fly fishing is a classier and more "sporting" way to catch fish. I find that trout taste just as good when caught with a worm on a hook. Fly fishermen look good; I'd rather eat well.

The area around Smalltown where I grew up is hilly—mountain country, actually. Consequently, every brook and stream is just teeming with squaretails. There's nothing like wading down a stretch of fast-moving water, wondering what kind of deep hole lies around the next corner. Plus, I feel like I'm contributing to the natural cycle of the food chain. I'm fishing for food, while the smart trout are stealing my worms for sustenance, and I'm providing a meal for the hundreds of hungry mosquitoes.

Some of my buddies prefer to troll around in a boat. They say it's because they can catch bigger fish that way, and I suppose that's true. I've gone with them at times and we've usually spent hours without so much as a bite. I'm pretty sure Barney and Roy like the lake fishing because it's conducive to drinking beer. They don't often catch trout, but they always catch a buzz!

Some of you might have heard of my uncle Herbert. He wasn't much of a sport; he fished for food, and paid little attention to the regulations of the Department of Inland Fisheries and Wildlife. Consequently, the local game wardens kept an eye on him.

The story goes that one Saturday morning Uncle Herbert was putting his twelve-foot johnboat into Pickle Pond when Warden Dain Eldridge arrived at the boat launch.

"You gonna play by the rules today, Herbert?" Warden Eldridge asked.

"Of course I am, Dain. You know I always do." He grinned, exposing his three tobacco-stained teeth.

"Then I guess you won't mind if I join you in your boat," the warden replied with a grin.

"Suit yourself, Dain. Just make sure you bring a life jacket; it's the law."

Uncle Herbert hadn't been on the lake for thirty minutes when he decided the fishing was too slow, so he moved on from Plan A to Plan B. He laid his spinning rod on the bottom of the boat and reached into his tackle box, from which he retrieved a small stick of dynamite. With little fanfare, he lit the fuse, tossed the explosive overboard, and reached for his long-handled net.

Within seconds, the fishermen felt a rumble under the boat and my uncle was scooping dozens of trout out of Pickle Pond and into his boat.

Warden Eldridge, of course, was appalled at Uncle Herbert's blatant disregard for the law and his authority.

"Herbert, what in the world are you thinking? You know you can't use explosives to kill fish. You know damn well I'm going to have to arrest you. You're gonna lose your license and pay a big fine. Have you lost your mind?"

Uncle Herbert didn't answer right away. Instead, he calmly reached into his tackle box, lit another stick of dynamite, and handed it to the warden.

"Now, Dain, are you gonna talk or are you gonna fish?"

The High Cost of Venison

IN 1962, DAD AND UNCLE JACK built a hunting camp in the mountains just a bit north of Smalltown. It's hard country; a hard place to hunt, and a hard place for deer to survive. Consequently, the deer numbers up near Island Lake are small, but those deer who survive are the biggest, the strongest, and the smartest of the land.

I still go to the deer camp each November, and I really do get out into the woods to hunt. My brothers K.C. and Sam and I bought out our Uncle Jack's interest in the camp years ago, but make no mistake about it, it is still Dad's camp.

In the past twenty years, given my limited success, the little woman has started to wonder if I take my .308 just for show. I've bagged two bucks, both large eight-pointers, and little else. I'm obviously not a meat hunter, and thank goodness Winnie and the kids never had to depend on me to put meat on the table. I'm a trophy hunter—that's my story and I'm sticking to it.

Two bucks in twenty years; I'm obviously not a great hunter. So how, you might ask, did I manage to outsmart two trophy bucks? Deer don't survive to reach the age and size of these bucks unless they are smart and strong. Smart, that is, for eleven months a year. In late November and early December, their brains relinquish control of their activities to their hormones. This phenomenon is not exclusive to the species

Deerus americanus. Just look at the intelligent, talented males of our species who have exhibited similar irrational, risky behavior. (Tiger Woods, Bill Clinton, and Senator Gary Hart come to mind.)

Trophy hunters, like me, pay a lot for venison. The little woman recently did the math for me:

- Camp taxes, utilities, insurance, and maintenance: $600 a year
- Food during the deer season: $300
- Beer and other adult beverages: $100 (at least)
- Gasoline for my Dodge half-ton (400 miles on back roads @ 6 mpg in 4WD): $264
- Hunting supplies: $300
  1. "Hot Doe" urine: has the same effect on old bucks as Estée Lauder on male Democrats (e.g., Kennedy, Kennedy, Clinton, Hart, etc.)
  2. Global Positioning System (in case I venture more than the usual 200 yards from camp)
  3. Grunt call: to simulate sound of hot females (see #1, re: male Democrats)
  4. Wool hunting pants (see #2).

Winnie's calculated cost of the venison I've harvested: *$150 per pound*.

The look on the little woman's face when I told her I agreed with her, and I'd decided to quit hunting as a hobby and start collecting expensive, vintage Corvettes instead: *Priceless!*

Weathermen Don't Know Sleet

I'M GUESSING METEOROLOGISTS go to college for at least four years; some of them for six or eight, I'm sure. So why, with all their schooling and all their high-tech gizmos, are they accurate about half the time?

There are several, well-funded federal and international agencies sending up weather balloons as well as geostationary and polar satellites, and using Doppler and polarimetric radar to predict the weather, and still we get some genius on the evening news telling us: "Tomorrow will be mostly sunny, except if it rains or snows."

My eighty-four-year-old mother-in-law is more reliable than all of them. She never had the opportunity to attend college, but when I want to know whether to wear my HUNKA HUNKA BURNIN' LOVE tank top or my raincoat to the pig races at the county fair, I call her.

The TV weather personality may predict mostly sunny skies, but if Bea says "Red sky in mornin', sailors take warnin'," I'm wearing my high rubber boots.

The scientists study El Niño and La Niña patterns to predict long-range weather patterns and try to warn us about how much snow to expect in January. I've learned to pay little attention to their predictions, but if my mother-in-law tells me the squirrels have been loading up on extra acorns and beechnuts all November, I'm going to see my buddy, Barney, to buy a forty-eight-inch, thirty-horsepower snowblower.

I don't pay any attention to Punxsutawney Phil on Groundhog Day. Seems like every year he sees his shadow on that early February morning and we are told to expect six more weeks of winter.

First off, where I live, a winter that ends in late March is something to celebrate. I've seen my brother K.C. do cartwheels down Main Street wearing only his BVDs after news like that.

Secondly, of course Phil sees his shadow every Groundhog Day. He pops out of his hole and is immediately greeted with the flash of two hundred cameras and five gazillion megawatts of TV camera lights. It could be midnight and he'd see his shadow.

My little woman's mother is a veritable encyclopedia of rhyming weather predictions:

When dew is on the grass, no rain will come to pass.
When leaves show their back, rain we won't lack.
When the wind is from the south, rain is in its mouth.

Still, my father-in-law, Floyd, hasn't learned to rely on his wife for weather advice.

Floyd has been farming for over fifty years. One late August morning he really wanted to cut a field of rowen hay before the weekend. Rain was predicted for the entire week to follow.

"Bea, I'm going to mow the Quimby Field today," Floyd announced at the breakfast table.

"The cows are lying down," she replied.

"So?"

Bea hardly looked up from her bowl of shredded wheat. "It's gonna storm today. You'll never get that hay dry, and it'll rot in the field."

Floyd bristled. He really wanted to cut that hay. "That pretty little girl, Sarah, on Channel Three promised sun today and tomorrow," he said.

"The cows are lyin' down," Bea repeated.

"They're just tired, you silly old woman. Sarah's a college-trained meteorologist—and she's some cute, too."

"Suit yourself."

Needless to say, Floyd had no sooner knocked down forty acres of valuable second-crop hay when the skies opened. It was the kind of weather that inspired Noah to build that big boat. The storm made mud so fast that my father-in-law soon had his Massey Ferguson stuck to the hubs of its five-foot wheels. It took two other tractors three hours in torrential rain to extract Floyd from the quagmire.

It was six o'clock that evening by the time Floyd, tail between his legs, dragged his sorry-looking, waterlogged, manure-enriched, mud-covered self into the farmhouse.

"What a day," he lamented. "I'm tired, dirty, cold, and starving. What's for supper?"

Bea was less than sympathetic. "I don't know, Floyd. Why don't you call that pretty little girl on Channel Three and ask her? Maybe she'll take you for a picnic on the beach . . . Don't forget your sunscreen."

My poor father-in-law didn't get a beach picnic or a home-cooked meal that night. In fact, he survived on humble pie for the following week or so.

Still Hunting (After All These Years)

THERE'S NO NEED TO LOOK AT THE CALENDAR to know it's
November in northern New England. Madison Avenue may
have its Fashion Week, but up north, we have November, our
Fashion Month. Just as the hardwood trees become naked and
stark and the grass turns to brown, blaze-orange hats, jackets,
and vests emerge from nearly every pickup truck and SUV.
It's rifle season for whitetails, and the rugged men and women
of the North Country dress for the occasion. Men who
haven't stepped foot into the woods in twenty years don their
bright-orange garb and hang a rifle in the back window of the
truck—just in case.

For those who actually get out and scare some deer, there
are three basic tactics: walking, sitting, or still-hunting.

Walking is a good way to see deer—very briefly—but an
almost impossible way to shoot one.

Sitting, or stand-hunting, is a technique which involves
sitting or standing in one location—ideally one in an area
known for heavy whitetail traffic (and close to camp)—in
hopes of ambushing a deer on its way to feed, breed, or just
lie down. This can be an effective method, but requires lots of
patience and a large quantity of Twinkies, teriyaki jerky, and
Twix bars.

Finally, there is my favorite—still-hunting—which is really
a hybrid of the two previously described tactics. Still-hunting

involves moving slowly, and hopefully quietly, through the woods, sometimes taking a half-hour or more to cover a hundred yards, in hopes of sneaking up on an unsuspecting buck.

In the early sixties, my father and uncle (that's two separate men, by the way) built a hunting camp in the big woods near Island Lake, about twenty miles north of Smalltown. Dad was a great hunter and my uncles were decent, too. The interior walls of our cabin are covered with twenty or so large racks of antlers taken from Buck Mountain. To this day, hunters drive miles out of their way to stop by our camp, just to rub shoulders with the Smalltown Boys, as we've come to be known.

A quarter-mile down the gravel road that leads to the Wright Boys Camp is the camp of our rivals, the Lebel Boys. The Lebels' camp is covered on the outside by dozens of small racks, a few of which were probably taken in daylight. The Lebels are a bunch of deer-poaching braggarts, and the Wright Boys hate them.

One cold morning, after climbing to the top of Buck Mountain, I was creeping along slowly through a thick patch of softwoods when I snuck up to within ten feet of a giant of a man before he heard me.

He was startled and embarrassed when he finally saw me, and asked a foolish question. "Are you still-hunting?"

"Well, I climbed all the way up this mountain; it seems silly to quit now," I replied.

Paul Bunyan didn't laugh. "I'm Lou Lebel. You've probably heard of me."

"Nope, can't say as I have." I wasn't about to give a Lebel the satisfaction of thinking their family was well-known in these parts. "So, Lulabelle, do you have a last name?" You see, I'm missing that filter that keeps most people from saying things that could lead to a good whoopin'.

"It's Lebel . . . Lou Lebel." He wasn't amused. "Who the hell are you?"

"Joe Wright."

"Oh, you're one of the Smalltown Boys," he replied.

"Yup. I guess we're famous around here." I grinned and walked away, thankful for the thick woods and my .30-06.

Things I Learned on a Fishing Trip

EACH SPRING I GO ON A FISHING TRIP to northern Maine with a bunch of my buddies. This year, we traveled to Millinocket, then over the Golden Road to the Teles Road, and rented a rustic cabin on Spider Lake. We fished Spider Lake, and the many brooks and streams that crossed our path, for brook trout. On Saturday, we spent six hours driving, two hours fishing and swatting deerflies, and three hours emptying our coolers of the various liquid and solid provisions we'd packed for a hard day of trying to provide food for our families.

Here's what I learned: My friend, Boozie, could fish in an aquarium containing a thousand trout and still catch and release the only chub (trash fish) on three consecutive casts. Jimbo, a rookie on the trip, is a good guy and is very bright— a veritable encyclopedia of useless information—until you get a pint of Crown Royal into him. Then, he's even stupider than the rest of us.

There are a lot of regulations pertaining to the taking and possession of brook trout in Maine. It seems that every body of water has its own rules. We studied the 300-page summary provided by Maine's Department of Inland Fisheries and Wildlife, and were still confused. We think we could keep up to five brookies over six inches, from brooks and streams, except those which are part of the Allagash Wilderness Waterway, in which case the trout had to be over twelve inches and we could keep only two fish, of which only one could be over fourteen inches, and each must have a notch in the dorsal fin, unless there were at least thirty-five orange spots on each side of the fish, except for fish in streams crossing the American Realty Road, which must have no more than twenty-five orange spots on each side. We think we obeyed the laws. My friend Barney has hired a lawyer to review the regulations and get back to us prior to next year's trip.

Another observation is that five-inch trout will always swallow the hook to their bellies, whereas twelve-inchers will be hooked by just enough of their lip to allow you to land them on the shore, where they will slip off and flop around in a half-inch of water while the fisherman tries, in vain, to grab the slippery trophy before it escapes back into the stream. The event, inevitably, results in a wild dance, an escaped fish, and a frustrated fisherman with a hook through his thumb.

There is a lot of wildlife in the northern Maine woods. We saw several moose, a few deer, and hundreds of rabbits. We counted 108 cottontails on our drive back to camp one evening. Apparently, they really do #$@%*& (reproduce) . . . like . . . well . . . rabbits.

I also noticed that beer seems to evaporate in a cooler while I'm fishing. It seems that Barney and Roy fish faster than I do, and they'd always be waiting for me at the truck when I'd climb out of the brook. They seemed really happy, even though several of our beer cans had apparently burst and were now empty. I'm not too bright, but I figured out by noon that

I'd been appointed the DF (designated fisherman). Have you ever been too drunk to fish? My buddies have.

There's something else I didn't know. It seems that the spare tire stored under the bed of a pickup truck is not intended to be actually used. We passed three trucks with flat tires on logging company roads. I think it is Murphy's thirty-seventh law which says that you can drive your truck around town for a hundred thousand miles on old, bald tires and never have a flat, but get into the woods a hundred or so miles, and you will finally need that spare, which is now cor- roded to the bottom of your truck.

We met several members of the Pelletier family; you know, the guys made famous by the *American Loggers* TV show. We drove by their impressive logging company facility at Clayton Lake, and there was little sign of activity. (We later discovered the reason for the inactivity.) It's apparently the off-season for the TV show, and we met several of the loggers at their brand-new restaurant and gift shop down in Millinocket. They were busy signing posters and T-shirts, and were not looking nearly as dirty or tired as they do on *American Loggers*.

We had a great time, and I'm hopeful we didn't inadver- tently poach any brookies with too few orange spots. To be safe, we ate them before they could become evidence.

I Don't Like Spiders and Snakes

I'M NOT A LITTLE GUY. I'm the best part of six feet tall, and I tip the scale at around two hundred. I was never the ruggedest guy in a barroom and I didn't like to fight, but with a buddy like Barney, it happened. Because if, Heaven forbid, some former NFL linebacker should look at Barney's woman, Jeannie, the wrong way, we'd have no choice but to pick a fight with "Bruiser" and his buddy "No Neck," both of whom were, at all times, teetering on the brink of steroid rage.

So you'd think, after repeated beatings as a younger man, I'd fear nothing. Nope. I squeal like a little girl at a Justin Bieber concert at the sight of a spider or a snake. I don't know why, as a grown man, I've developed this arachno-slithero-phobia. As a kid, I'd catch tarantulas and keep them in jars. And when I was thirteen, I'd capture garter snakes and show them to Suzie Springer, because I thought she'd think I was cool and want to be my girlfriend. Like so many of my attempts over the years to impress the opposite gender, that didn't work out for me.

I thought my irrational fear of slithering reptiles was unique until I witnessed my friend Wes's reaction to an eight-inch redbelly on a camping trip. Wes is as rugged a man as I've ever known. His upper arms are as big around as my thighs, and his chest is thick. He was a Marine in the 1960s. The Vietcong chased him through jungles, fired bullets and grenades at him, and made his life generally miserable for over two years. He slept in the rain forests, which he shared with tigers, gorillas, and orangutans. After that experience, you'd think he wouldn't be frightened by much of anything.

So, you can imagine my surprise at Wes's reaction to the tiny, harmless snake which wandered nonchalantly onto our campsite as we were cooking s'mores over an open fire. My son Jake was eleven at the time, so he was all over trying to catch the colorful little reptile, which proved to be quite adept at avoiding capture by a preadolescent boy. In Jake's defense, he, like the rest of us there, was a bit disturbed by the sight of a 300-pound man standing very precariously on a folding lawn chair while screaming in a high-pitched voice, "Get him, you little coward!"

Jake turned to Wes and shot him a look that clearly said, "You're calling *me* a coward?" The little snake used the opportunity to evade his pursuer and head straight for Wes's chair. Whoever coined the phrase "White men can't jump" didn't witness the ensuing three-foot vertical leap that led to a flattened lawn chair, a crushed reptile, and a rubber-legged, ghost-white, hyperventilating mountain of a man.

I have to admit, I feel a little better about my own aversion to cold-blooded serpents since witnessing Wes's response. I can't imagine jumping that high unless the little woman, Winnie, told me to.

Things I Learned Last Deer Season

I LIKE TO HUNT THE NORTH WOODS for the elusive white-tailed deer. There are more deer running around in the woods and nice, flat fields (including my lawn) near my home than in the mountain forests, but I hunt where Dad and Uncle Jack built our camp almost fifty years ago. That's where my dad, brothers, and friends go, and it's all about camaraderie—and beer and poker. Consequently, as I've admitted before, I'm not a very successful deer hunter. In fact, it would be more accurate to describe what I do as deer scaring rather than deer hunting. I sometimes make a few whitetails run really fast, but I infrequently kill one.

I've been going up to camp every November for forty-nine years now, and still I learn something new every season. Here's a summary of last year's lessons learned.

Firstly, *My instincts are not more dependable than my compass or GPS.*

I was sneaking (crashing) through a thick, softwood swamp when I decided it was time to head back to camp. After all, it had been three hours since breakfast, and I was all out of Twix bars. My compass and Global Positioning System agreed I should head west, but I've been hunting those woods since before the invention of GPS and knew I needed to head east. My navigational devices must have been rendered stupid by the magnetic strip on my Small-Mart credit card, which I carry with me in case I have a hunting emergency and happen to step out of the woods near a major shopping center.

So, following my instincts, I found myself on the Old County Road, three miles *east* of camp.

Navigational lessons learned:

- Many trees look alike, especially when you are lost.
- The moss grows on *all* sides of a tree when you are lost in a dark cedar swamp.
- It is impossible to use the position of the sun to find your way out of the woods during a blizzard, or after sunset.

Another thing I discovered last season: *The capacity of my bladder exceeds twelve ounces.*

I try to give myself every advantage when it comes to deer hunting. So, last year I bought a sixteen-foot, ladder-style tree stand and mounted it on a big old maple tree near my favorite deer runway.

I've read studies that indicate the whitetail nose is ten thousand times more sensitive than that of a human, which explains why one rarely sees a deer near a bait shop, sewage treatment facility, or paper mill.

Every season, I spend over $50 on scent-control products. I use Whitetail Research Laboratory's scent-elimination laundry detergent, dryer sheets, body soap, shampoo, and clothing spray, as well as fox urine cover scent to ensure that I will fool the most discriminating deer nose.

On the long-anticipated first morning of deer season, after two hours in my tree stand and a thermos of Green Mountain dark roast hazelnut coffee, nature called. Not to worry, though, knowing I wouldn't want to climb out of my tree stand to relieve myself, I was prepared, which is how I learned three lessons regarding scent control:

- The capacity of my bladder does, indeed, exceed that of a twelve-ounce Gatorade widemouthed bottle.
- It is impossible to stop the flow or control the trajectory and direction of one's pee while standing sixteen feet above the forest floor on a windy day in November while holding a full Gatorade bottle in one's left hand.
- There isn't enough fox urine in the world to cover the scent of human urine on one's hunting pants and rifle, a ladder stand, and the leaves covering the ground below.

Finally, I figured out last season that *Deer do not like to run around on blustery days.*

I recall, when I was a kid, my father would wake my brothers and me before dawn on a morning when the snow was blowing sideways.

"Dad, we're not going out in this weather. It's a waste of time," I'd declare.

"Oh no, son, you're wrong," Dad would lie. "This is the best time to hunt. The big bucks are spooked by the squeaking and falling trees and run around with reckless abandon."

So, needless to say, we'd go out hunting . . . and see nothing but driving snow and crashing branches.

Last year, I finally figured it out. On nasty days, deer like a nice, warm, *quiet* place to hunker down . . . just like Dad.

Part IV: Family Matters

I'm Afraid of the Little Woman

As I've said, I weigh close to two hundred pounds. The little woman tips the scale at about a hundred and twenty, and I am scared to death of her.

Winnie and I have been together for a long time, so usually, when I say something stupid—which is, by the way, quite often—she just rolls her eyes and tells me I'm an idiot. Sometimes, however (and what makes my life dangerous is that there is no way to predict when this might happen), the little woman snaps, and my stupid comment sets off an estrogen-fueled tirade. This makes for a really hard day for old Joe.

Every Tuesday and Thursday evening, the little woman puts on a workout costume and tells me she's off to quilting class at the Smalltown Adult Education center.

Two weeks ago, I asked a simple question about whether her favorite pink sweatpants had shrunk across the backside, and the next thing I know, she muckles on to my wrist and I'm doing a midair 360 and landing on my back atop the kitchen linoleum while Winnie swears at me in Japanese.

Come to think of it, I haven't seen any new quilts around the Wright household. But a white bathrobe with a brown belt around it did appear in the little woman's closet recently. Is it possible they teach jujitsu at the adult education center?

I've never claimed to be smart, and I've figured out that I seem to be missing that brain-to-mouth filter which keeps most people from making the kind of insensitive remark that has, so frequently, led to a whoopin' for poor Joe—but recently I've had an epiphany. I believe that, on occasion, I've been poisoned.

Winnie prepares most of what I ingest, and I'm thinking it might be more than a coincidence that, on several occasions, my misunderstood or poorly timed remarks have been followed by a two- to three-day period during which my activities were limited to things I could do while within thirty feet of a toilet.

I'm not concerned that Winnie would poison me to death. After all, I do bring home a weekly paycheck. Furthermore, I don't believe in life insurance. Let's face it: A guy who's prone to saying stupid stuff shouldn't tempt fate . . . or the little woman.

Catspeak

THE LITTLE WOMAN'S CAT, Kitty, can speak. She doesn't converse in English, of course, but after years of living with her (as her faithful servant), I've come to understand her. Her vocabulary is limited to one word; it's the tone—the inflection—that conveys her meaning. After thirty-some years of marriage, I've become much attuned to the nuances of tone and inflection. It's a survival skill.

Kitty typically has little to do with me; she's Winnie's cat. However, she'll follow me to the kitchen every time I fetch a snack for myself, which is often.

"Go away," I'll snap at her. "I just gave you a can of Gourmet Ocean Fish Delight."

She'll reply with a quick, high-pitched *meow*. That's Kitty speak for "*You* try that crap. They ought to call it Mackerel Tongue, Tails & Entrails. Thanks for buying me the fancy stuff—twenty-nine cents a can. Woo-hoo. I wouldn't want you to have to share a bite of your eight-dollar-a-pound haddock fillet!" Kitty has a real flair for sarcasm.

Kitty likes to look good. She spends a lot of time primping and preening. Maybe she learned that from watching me. I'm concerned that she may have bulimic tendencies. Just the other day, I caught her with a paw partway down her throat. Shortly thereafter, I discovered a hardly digested pile of Gourmet Ocean Fish Delight on the living-room floor. It's always in the living room—the only room with carpet (beige). She won't vomit on the linoleum in the kitchen.

We've raised Kitty as an outdoor cat. She goes out often, which, of course, means she returns just as frequently, but never comes or goes when I'm standing near an exit. Oh no. It's always after I've settled in on the sofa under a warm blanket, enjoying an episode of *Two and a Half Men*, that she decides she wants to go out.

"I just asked you if you wanted to go out," I'll snap at her. She'll reply with an indignant *meow*, which I'm fairly certain translates to "I didn't want to go out then; that was seconds ago, you dummy. But I really need to go out now, and I'll scratch the side of your brand-new couch until you get your lazy self up and open the door for me!" Evil cat.

The old girl—the cat, that is—is starting to lose it, both physically and mentally. She likes to climb up onto the porch roof, but forgets that she has a hard time coming down. My response to her incessant whining—again, it's the cat I'm referring to—is that if she gets hungry enough, she'll come down.

So when this happened again last week, there I was, at Winnie's request, perched atop an extension ladder, trying to convince Kitty to let me help her down. She, of course, resisted my efforts to help her because . . . well . . . she just enjoys annoying me. I finally said, "Fine, stay up there then," and started my descent. Two steps down the ladder, Kitty lunged at me, landing, claws extended, on my face. She, of course, landed upon her feet on the hard, wooden deck. I didn't.

Meow, she moaned as she stood over my bruised and aching body. *Meow,* she repeated, telling me, "Get off your lazy keister and let me in, dirtbag. I'm hungry."

Winnie's cat is loudest at four a.m. when she wakes to prepare for a busy day of napping. *Meow,* she'll yell over and over until I get out of bed. *Meow* in this case means: "I don't really like you, but I hate to be up by myself, and besides, I might need a servant for something, so get up or I'll pee on your ten thousand–dollar Oriental rug."

Okay, my rug was made in Mexico and I paid $39 for it at Small-Mart, but I still get up to spend quality time with the little woman's cat.

My Beagle's a Dumb Dog

MY BEAGLE BOOZER is as dumb as a bag of rocks. He's a good boy and he aims to please, but he is stupid, even by hound-dog standards.

Boozer, like all hounds, is a sniffer. I'm fat because my only exercise is to take my dog for a walk once a day, and he won't walk more than five yards without stopping to investigate a tree, or a branch, or a leaf, with his overactive nose. I can only imagine what goes on in his little brain with each stop.

Oh, I'd better sniff that rock; it looks suspicious. Oh yeah, the neighbor's poodle Sophie peed on that rock two days ago. She thinks she's so special. I'll show her who's special. I may not have a rhinestone collar and a fancy haircut, but I'm just as good as she is. I'll just pee on the same rock. There, I did it. Take that, you hoity-toity French bitch (female dog).

Five yards later . . . *Oh, what's that smell on those leaves? I think it's a Big Mac. Someone threw a McDonald's bag here in 2011. I can still smell the two all-beef patties, special sauce, lettuce, cheese, pickles, onions on a sesame seed bun. Damn, I wish I'd been here three years ago.*

Boozer is a runner when he's not on a leash. Left to his own devices, he'd chase any other animal on four legs. God forbid a rabbit should cross our yard and hop into the adjacent woods. Boozer would chase that cottontail to Canada, howling all the way to the border.

That's why my beagle has to be on a cable run in the backyard. He's used that run for five years now and still hasn't figured out that he comes to a painful, abrupt stop when he reaches the end of his rope. *Geez, what happened? I was running so fast. I was closing ground on that cat in a hurry . . . almost had her this time.*

The neighbor's cat is a lot smarter than Boozer, and torments my stupid dog by running by him and stopping just beyond where his run will let him pursue her. Poor, stupid Boozer.

Thank goodness my hound dog sleeps a lot. It's the only time he's quiet. Boozer barks or howls at everything that moves. He barks at people, other dogs, squirrels, cars, horses, motorcycles . . . A falling leaf can elicit a howling tirade that lasts an hour. And if the doorbell rings, the mighty watchdog, who didn't hear the visitor pull into the dooryard or slam their car door, goes off like a four-legged burglar alarm. Poor, dumb dog.

Boozer isn't a drinker as his name might imply, but he certainly is an eater. He eats anything. He doesn't care if it's meat, vegetable, plastic, or metal. He's passed more metal than an inspector at Smalltown Tool & Die. I can't tell you how pleased I was to pay the veterinarian $800 for a procedure to retrieve the metal and plastic voice box of my grandson's Tickle Me Elmo from my hungry dog's gut.

You may be wondering why I'd keep such a stupid dog. I've often asked myself that very question. I guess it's because his love is unconditional. He's always glad to see me. I get home from work and he howls with delight, wags his tail, jumps on my lap, and thoroughly licks my face. It makes me feel good . . . even if he does eat his own frozen poop.

Childbirth Can Be Painful

WHEN JAKE, OUR FIRST CHILD, was born over thirty years ago, the little woman and I were, needless to say, quite excited. We did all the right stuff and read all the right books to be sure we were totally prepared for the parenting experience. Don't laugh yet; it gets funnier.

One of the things we did was to take a Lamaze course so that our little bundle of joy could enter this world in a natural, drug-free way. Winnie was about five months along when we started our classes, and while I thought I'd already done my part to get her to that point, I agreed to attend.

So, every Monday night for a month, we sat in a circle on the floor of the Smalltown High School gymnasium and practiced heavy breathing. There were deep, "cleansing" breaths and quick "hee hee hoo" breaths (for those untrained readers, that's "hee hee hee hee hee hee hee hoooooooo"), all designed to, I think, calm the expectant mother and entertain the expectant father. It seemed to me that the delivery was going to sound a lot like the conception, but, being a sensitive guy, I kept that to myself.

I had my doubts about how effective all that huffing and puffing was going to be, and it concerned me, a bit, that I was missing TV coverage of four Red Sox games for Lamaze classes. But, as I was learning, parenthood means sacrifice, and I was determined to do my part. So, I listened to the games through a hidden radio earphone. Winnie wasn't too proud of me when I yelled "Yes . . . yesssss!" in response to a Yastrzemski homer, just as the rest of the class was exhaling "hee hee hoo" breaths. Oops.

I did pay enough attention so that I became quite adept at "hee hee hoo" breathing (which is, by the way, also helpful for belly pain after an all-you-can-eat bean supper down at the American Legion Hall).

Finally, the big day came, and as soon as the Patriots game was over, I drove the little woman to the hospital. ("Remember, honey, Dr. Braley said most couples get to the hospital too early. We don't want to inconvenience him by arriving before we need to, do we?")

I helped her with the heavy breathing every ten minutes or so, and for the first three hours of Winnie's labor, the Lamaze techniques were working fairly well. That all changed in the final moments before the blessed event. There I was, inhaling deeply and puffing away, and, as always, being generally supportive, when it all fell apart. The little woman seemed to be in a bit of pain, so I did what I'd been trained to do.

"Breathe, honey, breathe. Hee hee hee hee hee hee hee hoooooooo," I coached her.

"You breathe, you idiot! You did this to me! Get me some drugs—*now!*—or you'll never touch me again!" she yelled. She hadn't been so mean or looked at me with those scary, Linda Blair *Exorcist* eyes when we'd practiced these relaxation techniques at home.

Thoughts of an Average Joe

I knew she didn't really want those unnatural drugs. "Just breathe, honey. It can't hurt that much. Lots of women do this every day."

It seems that wasn't the best choice of words.

Winnie got her drugs and everything worked out all right. We have some lovely photographs to prove it—group pictures of a tired mommy with sweaty hair, wrinkled-up baby Jake, and a proud daddy with a black eye.

Out of the Mouths of Babes

IF YOU'VE RAISED A CHILD, it's a sure thing that your precious little darling has embarrassed you in public by saying aloud what most adults might think, but never mention. It seems we are born honest, and it takes our parents several years to train that character flaw out of us.

The little woman had one grandmother who ascribed to the "Kids should be seen and not heard" philosophy. A visit to her Grammy London's house was not a good time. Winnie and her sisters were expected to sit on the sofa, legs crossed and hands resting gently on their laps. They were to speak only when spoken to, or otherwise become the target of a stern lecture about ladylike behavior and proper manners. Grammy London was not a fan favorite.

Nonetheless, when our children were young—Jake was six and Maggie was three—Winnie thought they should meet their great-grandmother before it was too late. About fifteen minutes into the visit, during which the children had been asked to sit quietly at least half a dozen times, Maggie asked her mother a good question. In a voice loud enough to be heard by Grammy London, and maybe the upstairs neighbors, Maggie queried, "So, Mommy, what's so great about Great-Grammy London, anyway?" It's a question that has gone unanswered to this day.

Many years ago, when Jake was four years old, I had advertised a camper for sale in *Uncle Hank's Trading Post*. Pete, from Waterford, had come over to check it out on a Thursday evening, and seemed interested. Jake had, apparently, overheard me express optimism to Winnie later that night.

On Saturday, when Pete returned with his wife for another look, he noticed that Jake was following him closely as he showed the Coachmen to his spouse. Finally, Pete's curiosity got the best of him. He asked my son why he was following so closely, and also, apparently, trying to smell him.

"Have you been sniffing me, son? Do I smell funny to you?"

Jake smiled at Pete and explained. "Oh no, sir. It's just that last night I heard my daddy tell my mommy that you smelled like money."

Pete didn't buy my camper.

Kids seem to save their most embarrassing commentaries for crowded restaurants. My brother K.C. tells the story of a trip to Denny's with his kids.

His boy Eli is very curious, observant, and . . . loud. About halfway through his Moons Over My Hammy breakfast, K.C. lost his appetite when Eli blurted out the obvious. Just as the waiter delivered meals to the family in the booth next to theirs, Eli said, "You're right, Daddy—those fat people shouldn't eat all those pancakes."

"Eli, I didn't say that," K.C. whispered.

K.C.'s wife Renée says his face changed from tomato red to frightened white within seconds. It got worse.

"But Daddy, you said 'No wonder they're so fat' when they both ordered The Big Stack."

I guess K.C. left $25 and half his family's food on the table and made for the door, Eli crying as they left.

"But Daddy, I'm not fat—why can't I finish my waffle?" he screamed.

Kids . . . you gotta love 'em.

My Daughter Is Getting Married

MY DAUGHTER MAGGIE IS GETTING MARRIED this summer, and
I'm here to tell you that things have changed—a lot—since
the little woman, Winnie, and I tied the knot in 1977. The
Wright household is all atwitter with excitement over the
wedding plans, and, while I have offered a few suggestions, it
has become readily apparent that my expected participation,
at this stage, is to write checks and stay out of the way.

I thought Winnie and I had a wonderful wedding and reception thirty-three years ago. After exchanging vows at the Smalltown Congregational Church, we were off to celebrate at the
Bull Mountain Ski Lodge. We had a great meal we picked up
at the Smalltown IGA—tuna- and chicken-salad finger sand-
wiches, IGA potato chips, and macaroni salad—served on paper
plates, the fancy ones with the little blue flowers on them.

It was quite a party too. We danced the night away to the
Rusty Bean Music Machine. (Rusty was a mechanic who moon-
lighted as a wedding singer.) Accompanied by his Casio key-
board, he belted out the nuptial classics, from Roy Orbison's
"It's Over" to the Rolling Stones' "(I Can't Get No) Satisfaction." I thought Rusty just might play something appropriate
for the occasion when he invited us to the dance floor as he
played the lovely Beatles ballad, "I Will." My new bride was
less than impressed, though, when he completed the Fab Four
medley with "I'm a Loser" and "I Should Have Known Better."

It was a great party, and before we knew it, we were dragging Schlitz cans behind our 1972 Chevy Vega on our way to honeymoon for two glorious nights at the Buck & Doe Lodge in Island Lake.

Now that Maggie is planning a wedding, I'm discovering that some entrepreneurs have found hundreds of ways to turn marriage into a major industry.

There are no more do-it-yourself weddings. One must hire a wedding planner for fear that the bride and her mother will forget some of the ways to spend money on the big event.

Maggie is a beautiful, wonderful, young lady, but she's pushing thirty—old-maid material by 1970s standards—so I was happy to agree with the little woman that our little girl should have a nice wedding. I had no idea what I was agreeing to.

Let me provide you with a partial list of the components of a twenty-first-century wedding.

- *An engagement party:* Because the bride's parents aren't going to spend enough on the wedding itself.
- *Save-the-date cards:* These go out several months prior to the invitations, just in case one person didn't hear about the impending nuptials via e-mail, Facebook, or Twitter.
- *The bride's dress:* Must be custom-made by a designer to ensure that it is like no other and costs as much as an entire 1977 wedding.
- *Music:* No Rusty Bean Music Machine. One must hire different musicians for the ceremony, cocktail hour, and reception. The band for the reception must include

a horn section and a lead singer with at least one
Grammy on his/her mantle. The cash outlay for music
on the big day must be equal to, or greater than, twice
the cost of the bride's dress.

- *Flowers:* Must include exotic species only; nothing grown
  in this country, and certainly nothing the father of the
  bride can pronounce . . . or afford.
- *Photographer:* Must include still photos and HD video.
  The photographer must be a descendant or former stu-
  dent of Ansel Adams, and must be so busy that he/she
  couldn't care less if you turn down their offer to docu-
  ment the big day for the cost of a European vacation.
- *Guest gift bags:* This is the item that earned me the nickname "George Banks"—you know, the Steve Martin
  character in *Father of the Bride.* I'm told we have to give
  each guest staying at the hotel a gift bag containing
  bottled water, aspirin, and snacks. *Pleeease!* I love these
  people, but will they really need snacks after the $150
  meal? And aspirin because I bought them too many $10
  cocktails? And water? Doesn't that come out of that
  shiny thing hooked to the sink, like at home?

I love Maggie, and I hope she is happily married for many
years. Her mom and I have been in a state of continuous bliss
for thirty-three years now. If wedding expense is a happiness
factor, I figure she and Rudy should be good for at least 330
anniversaries.

My Grandfather Shouldn't Have Driven

I REMEMBER WHEN I WAS A KID, my grandparents would come to visit and my dad would always ask the same question when they'd arrive.

"How was your trip?"

"Great," Grandpa would answer. "Your mother drove all the way. All I had to do was hold onto the steerin' wheel."

It got funnier every time, or at least you'd think so, to hear my male role models laugh. Little did they know at the time, twenty years later the story would be closer to truth than fiction.

Grandma never learned to drive, but at eighty, she saw a lot better than Gramps, so together they were a really safe team. He drove and she told him when there were kids or puppies in the road. If that's not scary enough, consider that Grandpa didn't hear so well either.

As Gramps approached his eighty-fifth birthday, I took him to see Dr. Seymour, our family optometrist, and explained our dilemma. She completed the exam and explained that Grandpa was 20/60 in his best eye, which restricted him to driving in daylight, and only within twenty-five miles of home. I made a facial gesture that let the young doctor know I didn't think Gramps should be behind the wheel at all.

"Mr. Wright, I don't make the laws," she proclaimed in a tone devoid of empathy.

"I understand, Doctor," I replied. "You know, Gramps has a lot of free time. I'm sure he'd be happy to drive you to and from work each day." She declined.

So, for another two years, Gramps drove his 1988 Cadillac Seville to Dan's Market, Small-Mart, and St. Mary's Church. You'd have thought that pink behemoth had flashing lights and the word AMBULANCE painted on it, the way the other drivers in Smalltown scattered to get out of its way.

Gramps seemed to see numbers more easily than letters. One Monday morning, he was driving his sweetheart, my grandmother, to Small-Mart when he was pulled over by Howard Smith, Smalltown's finest (and only).

"Mr. Wright, do you know why I've pulled you over today?" Howard asked.

"Who do I look like, Carnac the Magnificent?" Grandpa sputtered.

"I clocked you at five miles per hour. I wondered if you were all right."

"I was doin' the speed limit, Howard. The sign by the diner says five miles per hour, and that's what I was doin'."

Howard removed his Smokey the Bear hat and chuckled. "The sign says five miles to Bull Mountain, Mr. Wright."

"I'm not headed to Bull Mountain, so why are you tellin' me that?" Gramps grumbled.

Officer Smith rolled his eyes and threw both hands in the air. "Just thought you'd like to know," he lied. "Have a good day, and be careful."

Not a week passed before Officer Smith had Gramps pulled over again. "Mr. Wright, you were doing thirty-five miles per hour in a twenty-five zone."

"Howard, the sign back there said thirty-five; I know it did."

"Mr. Wright, that's an advertisement for rooms at the Sleep E-Z Motel—they start at thirty-five dollars a night."

"We don't need a room, Howard. Mabel and I live just around the corner. Do you think we're kinky or what?" Grandpa replied.

Officer Smith just shook his head. "Okay, Mr. Wright, I'll let it slide this time. Just pay attention to the signs, all right?"

Two weeks later, Howard was parked behind the pink Cadillac again, blue lights flashing. As he leaned in to speak to Gramps, he noticed my grandmother looked quite distraught. Her blue hair was windblown, her face ashen, and her white knuckles were seemingly glued to the dashboard.

"Are you okay, Mrs. Wright?" Howard asked.

"She replied in a shaky voice. "Y-y-y-yes, Howard. Just a little scared. We just turned off Route 105!"

My Grandson's a Corker

I'M FINALLY A GRANDFATHER! Jake and his wife Jenna have given Winnie and me the most amazing grandson ever. We had to be patient a while longer than most of our friends, but it was well worth the wait.

Hanson is the most handsome baby boy ever born . . . really. I'm not just saying that because he's my grandson. He honestly is the most beautiful baby I've ever laid eyes on. I suppose, to many of you, that comes as no surprise. He is, after all, a Wright boy. As such, he's destined to grow up to be handsome and charming. Eventually, he'll thrill some lucky young lady and become her Prince Charming—her Mr. Wright. I'm not kidding, just ask Winnie.

Hanson is really smart, too. He can already count to one hundred and can sing the alphabet. Well, not out loud, of course. He doesn't talk yet. For crying out loud, he's only eight months old! Well, actually, he does say one word. When we're alone, he calls me Grampa, just as plain as day. *Grampa* is his first word! He doesn't say it in front of anyone else because, on top of all his other admirable attributes, he's thoughtful and sensitive. He doesn't want to hurt the feelings of his parents or grandmother.

Like his father and me, Hanson is a die-hard Red Sox fan. He had little choice, really. Jake is an even more avid BoSox devotee than I am, so Hanson was born with two options: He

could be either a Sox fan or an Orphan. Anyway, my grandson likes to watch the Red Sox on TV. His favorite player
is Dustin Pedroia. I think that's because he figures he'll be
Dustin's size in a couple of years.

Hanson's already quite an athlete, too. He can swing his
little plastic bat with power, and already throws a fastball and
a spitter (actually, it's more of a drooler).

I love to take my grandbuddy out for a walk. His stroller
rides and handles like a Mercedes E Class, compared to the
junk I used to push Jake and Maggie around in. Then again, I
think it cost as much as my first car.

I'm sure you're reading this and thinking I'm seeing Hanson
as perfect through the biased eyes of a proud grandfather.
That's not true. I'm being totally objective about my amazing
grandson . . . honest.

My friends, Barney, Roy, Ted, and Bert, were all grandfathers before me. Barney has three beautiful, charming grand-
daughters, and I know in his eyes they are the most wonderful
babies to grace this planet. Sorry, Barney, but that's just not
true. They are amazing, and maybe the most incredible baby
girls ever born, but they're not Hanson.

Roy, Ted, and Bert have grandsons. Roy calls his little guys
his grandbuddies, a term I think he coined, and I really like
(and am not ashamed to steal). My friends are all very proud
grandfathers, and each thinks his grandsons are the bright-
est and most athletic little boys ever. I hate to break it to you
guys, but you are each seeing your grandsons through the
biased eyes of a proud grandfather. You need to be objective,

like me. I have to admit that your grandsons are absolutely incredible, but the most amazing ever? Well . . . umm . . . no. That would be Hanson.

Last week, I was walking the little guy through the park in Smalltown, and you should have heard the comments from the ladies we passed.

"Oh, what a cutie. Look at that precious face and that little tuft of hair on his head! And he's such a chubby little guy. Look at that belly, and the dimples in his kneess. He's just adorable . . . and that baby! He's adorable, too.

My Sisters Were Trouble

WHEN I WAS SEVEN YEARS OLD and growing up in Smalltown, my friends were starting to get bicycles and train sets to play with. I got sisters—Vanessa, Kelli, and Darlene. Every two years, I got a new one. At the time, I'd have preferred a new Schwinn or Lionel, but I didn't get a vote. It seems Dad had more passion than money, so I got sisters.

So, what's a young boy to do? I tried to make the most of my situation. Mom had her hands full with all the housework and dirty diapers—there were no Pampers back then—and she was happy to send me out with a sister in a stroller. Sometimes I'd have to fight with my older brother Sam over who got to take the baby out for a ride; he'd figured out that the twelve- and thirteen-year-old girls on the street liked to play with the baby girls. I hate to say it, but when it came to getting the attention of adolescent girls, Sam needed every advantage he could muster. I, on the other hand, had no interest in romance at that time—I was into stroller *racing*.

Eastern Street, in Smalltown, is on a hill. It was ideal for racing my little sisters against Bubba Leonard's baby siblings. The contest rules were quite simple: There was a ten-yard push zone, a fifty-yard steep hill, and a chalked finish line where Bubba's brothers, Lennie and Peanut, would stop the speeding strollers. There was often a wager involving some marbles, a Baby Ruth candy bar, or an empty Donald Duck

Pez dispenser. For the first few years, I lost some good stuff to Bubba; his baby sisters, Lula and Trixie, were fat, and gravity gave them an advantage.

When Darlene came along, I got even. My youngest sister wasn't fat, but all the racing had worn out the old baby buggy, so my folks had bought a new one with bigger wheels and more mass. I did my part, too. The wheels were always greased, and I removed the sun shield to improve aerodynamics. By the end of the summer of 1966, I owned all of Bubba's marbles and half of his plastic army men.

I was a good kid, but I got into a lot of trouble with my parents because Vanessa was an instigator and a tattletale. She'd provoke me until I'd give her a gentle shove, and then, because she was awkward, she'd crash into Mom's favorite knickknack—the one she'd gotten with the S&H Green Stamps she'd earned at Dan's Market—and then knock it to the linoleum floor. As it turns out, Mom didn't go for the *Venus de Milo* armless-lady look, and I went without Oreos for a week.

Kelli was nearly as evil. She convinced me to peek into my parents' closet just before the Christmas of 1966 in exchange for three Lorna Doones. It was a deal with a five-year-old devil. I made the error of telling her what I saw there and she was so excited, she sang the "Hi Heidi" doll commercial nonstop at the dinner table that night. Once again, poor little Joey got busted, and it was me, not the instigating little sister, who washed dishes for a week.

Darlene was a bit easier on me, perhaps because I'm about eleven years older than she is, but I think she never squealed on me about the stroller races because she was so exhilarated by the speed and the thrill of victory, and because I shared the Baby Ruth bars with her.

Despite being a kind and protective big brother, I endured a lot of punishment as a boy because my little sisters liked to get me into trouble. I loved them just the same, and I still do.

I learned from those experiences and, as a result, I knew better than to punish my son Jake when Maggie told me he threw burdocks in her hair, kicked her, hit her, stole her lunch money, or duct-taped her to a tree and tortured her with a squirt gun . . . because I know how little sisters can lie.

My Uncle Bing Liked to Fight

His full name was Bingham Wright, but everyone except his mother, called him Bing. To me, he was Uncle Bing—my father's older brother—who, aside from my dad (Rufus Wright), was the man I admired most. My uncle could fix anything. He was good with wood, a wrench, and me.

Uncle Bing was one of a kind—a little tough to describe. He was built like Popeye, small and wiry, and had a bulbous nose and Alfred E. Neuman ears. His wispy red goatee looked like it needed fertilizer, and he played with it constantly.

Unk, as I called him (and most of my uncles), moved like he had twice as many joints as most people—kind of a herky-jerky motion reminiscent of the Scarecrow in *Wizard of Oz*. He was wound a bit too tightly and his motions were nearly constant. Unk was entertaining to watch, and even more comical when he was speaking, which was, seemingly, every waking moment. I recall, on several occasions, seeing my father shake his head incredulously as he asked his brother, "Bing, have you ever enjoyed an unspoken thought?"

Uncle Bing's language skills were limited, to say the least. He had a bit of a speech impediment, compounded by his New England accent and the apparent inability to talk without arm-flailing: "Don't go fwappin' yer wings at me," he'd yell at my angry aunt Gert, his thumbs tucked under his armpits and his own elbows aflutter. "Ya wook wike a woon in the watah."

Unk had his own vocabulary; Dad called it "Binglish." He would much rather talk than listen and, I'm guessing, paid little attention to how others pronounced their words. Dad called him "a poor man's Norm Crosby." Poor Uncle Bing never made his living using phrases like "self-defecating humor" (which, if you think about it, makes a certain amount of sense) the way old Norm did.

Unk liked beer—a lot. He really liked Miller High Life, but usually sucked down Old Milwaukee because it, like him, was cheap. His favorite beer, though, was O.P. (Other People's).

"Yes, pwease, I'd wuv a Bud Wight [or Miwwaukee's Best, Coors, Michewobe, Schwitz]. That's my favorite."

He could handle beer fairly well. Vodka was a different story. Pour a couple of shots of Popov into Uncle Bing and he'd lose all perception of his relative size, seek out the biggest man in the room, and pick a fight. He wasn't blessed with a sensitive brain-to-tongue filter to begin with. Add vodka, and the filter disappeared altogether.

Dad tells a story about a trip with Uncle Bing to the big casino down in Connecticut. "We were sitting for hours pullin' on the one-armed bandits, and I knew we were in trouble when the pretty little girls in the short skirts kept offering complimentary drinks. I heard 'Vodka Cowwins, pwease' about three times too many, and figured I'd be bailing Bing out of jail or a rumble before the night was over."

As fate would have it, 300 pounds of muscle, nicknamed Killer, parked himself at the flashing, dinging, "Jacks Are Wild" machine next to Unk. His big-boned, peroxide-blonde lady stood beside him. They wore matching HOG WILD black leather jackets, and she squealed with each 50-cent payoff. "Killer, you won again! You are so good at poker."

Dad says he knew Uncle Bing hadn't spoken to anyone other than the cocktail waitress for over an hour, and was getting antsy to strike up a conversation. He was sure that, considering his little brother was by then a Smirnoff-fueled talking and fighting machine, this wasn't going to end well.

Dad was right.

Killer had just won a $1.25 jackpot and Blondie was jumping for joy, various body parts bouncing about as she squealed. Unk slapped Killer on the back and extended his hand. "Good job! My name's Bing." Uncle Bing's hand disappeared inside his new friend's massive paw.

"Reggie Johnson. My friends call me Killer." He pointed to the name embroidered on his jacket, as Blondie giggled. "And this is my girl, Tiffani."

And that's when the trouble started. Unk tugged on his wispy chin whiskers as he looked Tiffani over. "Pweased ta meet ya, Tiffani. I ain't never seen a girl like you 'cept in a Pwayboy magazine."

Dad says Unk ducked just in time to avoid a haymaker that would have validated Reggie's nickname. Pops had all he could do to keep the big-boned blonde off his brother, and watched the show as he held onto 170 pounds of a Kahlúa-charged biker chick.

Unk bobbed and weaved and chattered as he kept just out of Killer's reach.

"I'm gonna crush you like a bug," the gorilla growled at my uncle, who was now moving like a cross between a Slinky and a pogo stick.

Unk, of course, couldn't keep his piehole shut. "Easy, Kiwwah, it was s'posed to be a compwiment. They only put pwetty girls in those dirty magazines."

"I'll show you pretty, you little cow flop!" Killer shouted.

Uncle Bing was moving like Gumby, but thought he was Muhammad Ali. "Fwoat wike a butterfwy, sting wike a bee," he taunted.

Dad was amazed at how fast Uncle Bing was moving and how slowly Casino Security responded to this impending homicide. "Stay out of his reach, Bing," Dad implored.

"Don't wowwy, Wufus, I know kwai tondo. One swift kick to the bwead biscuit, and he's goin' down wike a bag o' bwicks." Finally, three men in dark blue sport coats restrained Killer as two others chased Uncle Bing.

Uncle Bing made it through the dollar and quarter slots and past the penny machines, where he hurtled himself over a blue-haired lady in a wheelchair (causing her to crush her cigarette against her oxygen bottle) and past the roulette tables before Security nabbed him.

He was still sputtering as Dad helped him up from the puddle outside the casino. "I wooda made it outta there on my own if that bwackjack tabow weren't in the fweakin way!"

They broke the mold when they made my uncle Bing. He was irreplaceable, and although he's been gone for years, I still miss him today.

Go to Your Room

THE RULES OF CHILD-REARING have changed since I was a kid growing up in Smalltown in the 1960s and '70s. My grandson Hanson is only nine months old (and he's perfect), so he hasn't been the object of any significant parental discipline, but I'm sure that in spite of his inherited good nature and genetic predisposition to being a good boy—a Wright boy—his parents will occasionally have to remind him who's in charge.

I have, however, observed less-than-perfect children—spoiled little brats—misbehaving at Dan's Market and Applebee's, and, I must say, I'm sometimes shocked by their parents' reaction to the antics of their precious little darlings.

I don't spend a lot of time in the grocery store, but last week I stopped at Dan's to pick up a twelve-pack of my favorite malt beverage. What I saw there shocked me. Blue Ribbon in hand, I was in search of some fried pork rinds when I passed a young father and his three-year-old son in the cereal aisle.

"No!" screamed the toddler. "No Shredded Wheat," he said, transferring the box of wholesome cereal from the shopping cart to the floor. "I want Lucky Charms and Cap'n Crunch."

I have to admit that my knee-jerk reaction was, "I'm with you, kid. Those frosted Lucky Charms are magically delicious." But then, I heard the young dad's response as he placed the Shredded Wheat back in the cart, only to have it ejected again by his screaming kid.

"Now, Tristan, when we get home, you're going to have a time-out so you can think about how you're behaving," the young father calmly proclaimed.

I'm thinking, *Time-out . . . what in the world does* that *mean?* My father would have dealt with that kind of behavior promptly. I'd have been ejected from the shopping cart and Dad would have issued a less-than-gentle slap to my bottom, as well as a loud and clear message: "Joey, put the Shredded Wheat back in the cart . . . NOW! You'll eat Shredded Wheat. And if you don't, I'll fry up some pork liver for you." There'd have been no time-out, and I'd have quietly shared the shopping cart with tripe and canned spinach, too.

Two weeks ago, Winnie and I were at Small-Mart. I was checking out camouflaged hunting blinds when two young brothers started grappling over the one remaining grunt deer call in the store. At the height of the melee, one of the boys, who looked to be about five years old, used a four-letter word, followed by "you" to express his displeasure with his slightly older brother. (The four-letter word wasn't *love.*) Their mother, dressed in her best camo sweat suit, appeared from the next aisle, where she'd been studying the various doe-in-estrus buck lures, to address her younger son's behavior.

"Hunter, we don't use that kind of language in public," she said. "When we get home, we're going to discuss why you shouldn't use that word except at home."

Winnie looked at me in disbelief. All I could think was that as a kid, I wasn't allowed to use that word in public, in private, or even in my head! And there'd have been no discussion when we got home. My mom would have marched me right over to the soap aisle. It's difficult to discuss anything with a bar of Lifebuoy in your mouth.

My niece Jayne was nice enough to invite us over to her place last Thanksgiving. Her daughter, Chloe, is as sweet as can be, but is at that age where little girls don't always see eye to eye with their mothers (you know, from ages eight to twenty-one).

During the course of dinner, Chloe told her mom that the turkey was dry, the tablecloth was ugly, and finally—the comment that prompted her father to respond with unthinkable discipline—she told her mother she was stupid.

"Go to your room, young lady. And don't come downstairs until you are ready to apologize to your mother."

Chloe calmly rose from her chair, smiled, and retired to her room. At first I was surprised at how well Chloe had accepted the seemingly tough love. Then I remembered seeing her room earlier in the day. I've seen rooms in five-star hotels with fewer creature comforts. Well, actually, I've never stayed in a five-star hotel. I'm just saying Chloe's room has lots of amenities. There's an iPod with a Bose sound system, a flat-screen TV with hi-def and 300 cable channels, a laptop with wireless Internet service, and a mini fridge stocked with ice cream and cake.

I like hi-def TV and I love cake and ice cream, so I thought of telling my niece Jayne that she was stupid. But her husband Kirk is freakishly strong, and I was afraid he might respond with something other than "Uncle Joe, go to Chloe's room."

Baby Camp

Our grandson Hanson is ten months old now, and as I've mentioned, he's a real corker. My son Jake and daughter-in-law Jenna take good care of Hanson, which has caused some of us to covet his lifestyle.

Jake's buddy, Lew, came up with the idea for a business venture called Baby Camp. The premise is simple: Adults, like me, could pay for a stay at a resort and be treated like babies. I think I'd sign up for Baby Camp.

Such a vacation facility would be staffed by young people—twenty- to forty-year-olds—people of childbearing age. The women would be cute . . . well . . . because it would be good for business. The men would be handsome, for the same reason, and would be big and strong, so that when a guy my size gets fussy, the male staff members could carry me around and pat me gently on the back.

I'd be fed from a really big bottle with a soft rubber nipple. Since I've been over a year old for quite some time now, I could have milk products (vs. formula), and, in fact, I could have flavored milk products—chocolate, strawberry, Kahlúa, White Russians . . .

I could leave my teeth at home, because cute little "Mommy" staffers would feed me plenty of soft foods while I sat in a giant high chair. I'd enjoy *pâté de foie gras*, coffee ice cream, chocolate pudding with whipped cream, and mashed potatoes with lots of butter. (I'd sign up for Fat Camp right after Baby Camp.)

I'd get lots of naps. I'm pretty sure the camp staffers would encourage me to sleep a lot. And I wouldn't have to worry about getting out of my massive crib when Mother Nature called. I'd be wearing a nice, soft, cotton diaper, and when I got up from my nap, a Baby Camp Mommy or Daddy would really earn her/his wage. (That's why they'd make the big bucks.)

I think the best part of Baby Camp would be the ability to summon complete attention to my needs with a simple whimper. When I needed a drink, some ice cream, or a hug, all I'd have to do is cry or whine a little and someone would be there to take care of my every whim.

I'd like the baby talk, too. "Oh, little Joey, you are so cute! Look at that chubby little belly and those chunky little thighs! You are sooo adorable and sooo smart . . . yes, you are; yes, you are!" I'd like that.

Transportation would be easy, too. Baby Camp Daddy would carry me to the Baby Camp Hummer, where he'd strap me into a massive car seat and then he, or the mommy, would drive me to Cabela's and push me around the hunting and fishing departments in a giant stroller, equipped with fleece lining, really soft blankets, and an awesome stereo system.

I'm saving up for a Baby Camp vacation; I don't care what it costs. I could have fun at a place where I'm the boss, Baby Camp parents and grandparents are hired to spoil me rotten, and burps are cute.

Mothers Are Liars

BELIEVE IT OR NOT, when I was a kid I'd sometimes tell stories that didn't represent the truth, the whole truth, and nothing but the truth. As a result, when my mother found out that I'd stayed after school for shooting spitballs at Suzie Springer—and not because I'd volunteered to set up chairs in the auditorium for the annual Smalltown Elementary Stars and Stripes Variety Show, as I'd claimed—I'd get my mouth washed out with soap. I never liked that but, as a result of my childhood experience, I can tell you that Ivory tastes better than Lifebuoy, Lifebuoy better than Dial, Dial has overtones of citrus and industrial chemicals, Irish Spring was "Manly, yes . . ." but I didn't like it, and Lava had the flavor I'd expect of toxic waste, and was abrasive enough to sand all the taste buds off my tongue.

So, you can imagine my frustration when I figured out later in life that my mother didn't always tell the truth either.

"It was for your own good, Joey." That was her justification. "It wasn't really a lie; it was just a little fib."

That's why it was okay for her to tell me I was really smart, and that the only reason Mrs. Wilson kept me in the third grade for three years was because I was such a good boy and she really liked me.

It was for my own good that she told me I was the best-looking boy in my fifth-grade class.

"But Peggy said I have buck teeth, freckles, beady eyes, and thick glasses," I'd explain.

"Well, that's true, Joey—those are the things that make you look like your father. You're a Wright boy, and in a few years you'll grow into that look, and all the girls will be fighting over you."

Turns out there wasn't a lot of fighting going on when I got to high school. Thank goodness I met Winnie, who has also, over the years, taken in a one-eyed beagle, a three-legged cat with the mange, three blind mice, and, when we were raising laying hens, a banty rooster with chronic laryngitis and erectile dysfunction.

I, like my father and his father before him, never grew into my looks. My mother had fibbed.

In my mother's defense, I've discovered that she's not the only child-rearing woman prone to distortion of the facts. I've heard Winnie tell some whoppers to our young ones over the years.

As luck would have it, Jake takes after the Londons more than the Wrights, so she didn't have to convince him he'd grow into his looks. However, he *was* certain of the existence of the Easter Bunny and the old man in the white beard and red suit—until he put it all together when Maggie leaked the truth about the Tooth Fairy after he crashed his bike and knocked out a front tooth at the age of thirteen.

That's not to say Maggie is less gullible than her big brother. She's over thirty now and still believes that thunder is caused by the angels bowling in heaven, and babies are delivered by the stork.

Mom, now that I'm grown with kids of my own, I understand why, at times, you lied to me. It's just like the time I told you that someone ran into your car in the Small-Mart parking lot, causing thousands of dollars of damage to your nearly new Impala while I was inside the pharmacy, picking up your thyroid medicine. It was for your own good, and it wasn't really a lie . . . just a little fib.

Part V: Things that Confuse Me

Where'd This Tattoo Come From?

Did you every wake up with a headache and some new body art? Me, neither . . . honest. I was just wondering about you. This isn't about me, is it?

As I look around at the epidermis of my friends and neighbors, I'm seeing an investment opportunity that in ten to twenty years will fund my retirement and allow Winnie and me to buy that new motor home we've been dreaming of. I'm going to develop a tattoo-removal system that is painless, effective, and *very* expensive. The way I see it, there will be a lot of future parents and folks going through that midlife change—you know, the one that makes "life in the slow lane" seem like a good thing—who will pay a lot to erase some body art.

"It seemed so awesome at the time," they'll say. "I didn't know I was going to get older, have kids, get divorced, have a career and stuff." I guess we all think we'll be the first to avoid aging and a responsible lifestyle.

The other day, the little woman and I were having ribs over at Applebee's when in comes a young couple, both dressed in nothing but black leather. Coincidentally, they both had hair dyed a shade of black that just doesn't occur in nature. They each had so many piercings, I had to peek after they took a swig of beer just to see if their faces leaked!

Their skin was ghost-white—a nice contrast to all that black—except for lots of very colorful body art. You've got to know that the young man with PHOEBE engraved within a heart on his face is someday going to marry a Susan or a Mary . . . *Ka-ching!* A down payment on our new Winnebago!

And Phoebe, with the snake tattoo running from her right shoulder, up her neck, above her upper lip, and onto her left cheek, will someday be a soccer mom and president of the PTA . . . *Ka-ching! Ka-ching!*

I'm guessing that Josh, who bags my groceries down at Dan's Market, will someday be Reverend Joshua McDonald, and regret the SEE YOU IN HELL tattoo with flames emblazoned on the back of his right hand . . . *Ka-ching*, Reverend, and God bless you.

Lori, the lovely young blonde who serves me my weekly double hot fudge sundae with whipped cream and nuts (I'm sorry, but I'm weak) over at Carly's Ice Cream will someday tire of explaining the bright green image of a seven-pointed leaf adorning the area just below the front of her neck to her second-grade students at Smalltown Elementary. "Liam, it's like I told Olivia last week: It's an oregano leaf . . . I don't know why your daddy laughed when you told him that." *Money, money, money, money!*

Ernie, the former Marine who sells me my Bud Light down at the Big Apple convenience store, will be in to see me. His girlfriend Marissa will tell him that she won't marry him until he has that naked girl removed from his arm . . . Show me the money, Ernie!

I think I'm on to something big. I might even start looking at yachts, or a little winter place in Barbados and maybe a
BMW convertible for Winnie. All I need is a name for my new
enterprise: Tats-Be-Gone? No Regrets? Mistake Eraser?

I Remember When Water Was Free

WHEN I WAS A KID growing up in Smalltown, if you'd have told me I'd someday be spending a buck and a half for a bottle of water, I'd have suggested you visit the state mental institution over in Waterboro. Heck, my dad wouldn't even spend that for a six-pack of Narragansett back then.

The other day, I paid 75 cents for air to inflate the tires on my pickup. It made me think back to the days when I'd ride my Schwinn over to Jake Cassidy's garage and fill up the tires. He had a bright red pumping station out by the street with a sign that read FREE AIR. I remember at the time thinking, *Well, what other kind is there?* Back then, I'd work for an hour stacking firewood for 75 cents. I'd be damned if I'd spend that hard-earned cash on air.

I guess in the 1960s Mom and Dad paid a little something for telephone service. I can remember they didn't pay as much as the wealthier families because we had a party line—a line we shared with Mrs. McManus, the busybody up the street, who could listen in on Mom's conversations with my aunt Clara. But we certainly didn't pay for television reception. It seemed magical to me as a kid that those moving pictures and voices of the *Lone Ranger* or *The Ed Sullivan Show* were just floating around in the air. All we had to do was turn the rabbit-ear antennas just right and the black-and-white images would show on our Sears and Roebuck TV set.

Now I pay $95 a month for 302 channels, and most of the time I still can't find anything worth watching. I pay an additional $15 a month so I can rent black-and-white DVDs of *The Lone Ranger* and *The Ed Sullivan Show*.

Still, it's the water for which I most resent paying. I live in the country and have a drilled well, so most of my water is free. My friends in the village have "town water," which means they pay for the water they drink, and then again to flush it after they strain it through their kidneys.

When my daughter Maggie was a teenager, she made pretty good money working as a waitress at The Loon's Cry, a restaurant that catered primarily to wealthy summer people from away. She told me once about haughty Mrs. Hathaway in her fur and diamonds, who rudely pushed away the ice water Maggie had poured for her, saying, "Take this away, girl, and bring me some bottled water—French bottled water."

"Yes, ma'am," Maggie replied as she took the lady's water glass. Two minutes later, Maggie returned to the pompous shrew with the same water in a fancier glass with a slice of lemon garnishing the rim. Mrs. Hathaway sipped the "new" water and proclaimed, "Now *that's* delicious water. It's Dom Pérignon, isn't it?"

"Why, yes, ma'am, it certainly is. You have a discriminating palate, don't you?" my little darling replied.

"I know good water."

In the end, everyone involved was happy. Mrs. Hathaway got her "French" water; my daughter's boss got $2 for a glass of tap water; and Maggie got the satisfaction of serving just desserts to a pretentious older woman who thought herself better and smarter than her little girl waitress from the backwoods.

I suppose some of the best things in life, like vindication, are still free.

The Trouble with Tools

I SEEM TO HAVE A HARD TIME USING TOOLS. I like puttering
with wood and, to a lesser degree, working on my truck, but
I'm not very good at either. There are so many tools for shap-
ing wood and working on machines and motors these days. I'd
love to have one of each, just in case, but that's not practical
or financially feasible.

As it is, I own a biscuit joiner (no, that's not for attaching
crescent rolls to one another), a pocket joiner, and a tapering
jig that I rarely use, but they are available if I ever need them.
I own several books which describe the *intended* use of many
tools. I'm considering writing a book of my own to explain the
resultant effect of these same tools in my hands.

A Skil Saw, according to the books I've purchased, is a portable device used to quickly and accurately cut stud boards
to length for building and framing. In my hands, a Skil Saw
is used to consistently cut two-by-four studs a quarter-inch
shorter than needed—never too long.

A tape rule is a metal ruler on a roll, sort of like duct tape,
which is used to measure objects to within 1/32 of an inch of
accuracy. My tape rule is consistently off by at least a quarter-
inch (see Skil Saw, above).

A table saw is very handy for cutting and ripping boards
lengthwise. It can emit long, thick wooden projectiles at a

velocity capable of skewering a cat. It is also bad for the job security of manicurists and guitar salesmen.

My socket wrench set would be handy if I could discipline myself to replace the sockets to their well-labeled spots in the carrying case. It would also be helpful if the nut I was trying to loosen was labeled with a size. As it is, though, I try different sizes on the nut until I find one that is barely too large, which results in a nut that doesn't budge, but now has lots of rounded edges. I use vise grips to finish the job of rendering the nut edges smooth.

A standard straight screwdriver is useful for removing the slot in a standard screw, and also the first few layers of skin from the palm of my hand. Stripped, straight-slotted screws can be removed with vise grips or pounded in with a big hammer. The big hammer, of course, can also be used to blacken the left thumbnail.

An oil filter wrench, as it implies, is intended to remove the oil filter from my Dodge truck so that I can save $7 by changing my own oil. Since the filter is very difficult to get to, that wrench hardly ever works. Not to worry, though, because I can drive a long screwdriver through the filter and turn it that way. When that method fails, I can use the tool I should have used in the first place—my telephone—to call Rusty down at Blake's Esso Station. For $70 (he hasn't gone up since last year, when he towed me for the same reason), he'll come with his wrecker and haul my truck to his place and then, for $20, change my oil.

A Penny for Your Thoughts

DO WE REALLY NEED PENNIES anymore? I mean, what is a penny worth these days? I'm old enough to remember when a penny would really buy something. As a kid, I could go to the Smalltown IGA store and buy not one, but two pieces of candy for a penny—Mint Juleps, Banana Splits, or Chocolate Chews. They were delicious, and would stick to your teeth for hours. I suspect they were so cheap because they were subsidized by the American Dental Association.

Stop and think about it: What can you buy for less than a nickel these days? I can think of hardly anything I can buy for less than a dime. So, why does the US Mint spend all the time and money to produce millions of pennies every year? Why not save the copper for important things, like .30-06 shells? It seems like those are becoming harder to come by these days.

I suppose without pennies, the marketing gurus would have quite a dilemma on their hands. They seem to think we're all idiots. We'll pay $3.89 for a gallon of gasoline, but we're not foolish enough to pay $3.90. No way.

They started making pennies when you could hire a person to work all day for a dollar. Now I can't hire the thirteen-year-old fifth grader next door (that's right—he's still in the fifth grade . . . again) to mow my lawn for more than ten minutes for a buck. So, what's a penny worth?

The little woman loves pennies. She'd hate to see them disappear. Hardly a day goes by that she doesn't stop to pick up a penny on the sidewalk. "See a penny, pick it up, and all the day you'll have good luck" she'll repeat with every copper treasure she discovers. It's no wonder she finds so many— they're worthless. Who's going to stop and pick one up if they drop it?

Last week we were visiting our daughter in Brooklyn, where the sidewalks are like dog-poop minefields. You have to watch your step. Of course, there's more than dog poop on the sidewalks. There's litter and gum and *lots* of pennies. Winnie picked up at least a dozen Lincoln heads while we were there. I'm not sure if she got any good luck as a result, but she did get worms. She hasn't told me so, but I've noticed she sits on the carpet and twirls around in circles, which is always a sure-fire sign for our beagle.

These days, the expression "A penny for your thoughts" is an insult. Heck, most newspaper editors are willing to pay nickels for Thoughts of an Average Joe.

I hope you've found this chapter thought-provoking and, at least, a little humorous. If not, send me a dime and a self-addressed, stamped envelope and I'll mail you the good stuff.

Heavy Kids

I WAS DRIVING TO WORK ONE DAY last winter and passed a group of middle school–age kids waiting for the school bus. What I saw there in that group of a dozen or so youngsters concerned me. I was left to wonder if our economy is even worse than I figured.

It was a chilly morning—I spent five minutes scraping a heavy layer of frost from the windshield of my F-150—but the young girls at the bus stop were standing there shivering in their little skirts and T-shirts. Was it possible their parents couldn't afford jackets? And the boys, they were obviously wearing hand-me-downs from their much older brothers. Their blue jeans were two or three sizes too big and had holes in the knees. Their pants were so big around the waist that zippers and pockets were halfway to their knees. Thank goodness their older brothers left them hooded sweatshirts, as well, that were also three sizes too large. My heart ached for those poor children.

The other thing I noticed about the twelve- and thirteen-year-olds at the bus stop was that about half of them were heavy . . . overweight . . . you know . . . fat. It caused me to reflect on my eighth-grade class at Smalltown Elementary School. I honestly don't remember any fat kids. Some were, of course, bigger-boned than others, but none were really fat.

Part of the reason for our relative physical fitness was that there was no school bus service in Smalltown. We all lived in the village, within a mile or so of the school, and walked. For me, it was a mile each way, and I, like most of my classmates, walked home for lunch each day. Lunch was ready and on the table when we got there because, for the most part, moms stayed home back then. So, all told, I walked four miles a day, back and forth to school. Add another three miles a day lugging around and delivering forty-three copies of the *Smalltown News*, and I burned off some Hostess Twinkies.

We didn't spend much time in the house in those days. Almost every little house or apartment was home to four or more of us rug rats, and the folks made certain we spent most daylight hours outside. I don't remember that being a problem. There was one channel on TV, and the shows were in black-and-white. There were no Nintendo, Atari, Xbox, or PlayStation games to play.

Our dads cleared a ball field in the lumberyard across the road from our home, and there were lots of neighborhood kids to make up teams for pickup games of baseball or football. Our parents had to keep an ear toward the field because the Brown boys liked to swear, and the Ouellette boys and girls liked to fight. When a fight would break out, those of us not involved in the melee would step back and enjoy the show, until my father or Uncle Jack would come over to break things up.

Swearing was a different story. When one of the Brown brothers would let fly with a four-letter expletive, all action would freeze, and all eyes would turn to the second window from the right on the second floor of the house across the street—the window of my mother's kitchen. The warning was always clear and always the same. "You boys clean up your language or you're going home, and I'll call your mother!" That was all it took. They knew my mother would make good on her promise.

We played hard and worked hard in those days, and few kids were fat. Still, today's kids have it all over us when it comes to the thumbs. Their thumb dexterity is nothing short of phenomenal. The facility with which they use their opposed digit to type a text message, surf through the 300 digital TV channels, or fire off an Xbox missile is impressive indeed.

I'm envisioning a singles bar in the year 2025, in which a hefty young lady waddles past two guys—each of whom is straddling two barstools. One guy turns to the other, fans himself with a beer-stained paper coaster, and says, "Whoa . . . nice thumbs."

Nicknames

A LOT OF FOLKS IN SMALLTOWN, especially men, go by a name other than that which appears on their birth certificates. On Eastern Street alone, we had a Peeno, a Nuckie, and a Frenchy, to name a few.

I've noticed that the use of nicknames is far more common in rural America than in our cities. I haven't spent much time in big cities, but wealthy men, like Thomas Sullivan and William Robert Howell, own vacation homes on Shadow Lake. I can tell you from experience that Mr. Howell doesn't go for being called Billy Bob.

Some nicknames are derived from a person's physical attributes. I suppose that practice applies mostly to guys, because most women don't care for labels like Porky or Sweathog or Potbelly. Men, on the other hand, consider their nicknames to be a badge of honor. (My flatulent buddy Stinky Groves is a case in point.)

I saw a couple of exceptions to the gender rule at the county fair a few years back. There were a couple of talented female entertainers performing there: Busty Galore and Booty Jackson. They had funny names but looked like nice girls.

A lot of nicknames seem to be abbreviations of either the person's first or last name. In Smalltown, Leonard Smith is known as Smitty, Albert Johnson is Johnny, and Munzie Munson's real name is Eugene. Roosevelt Grier was 300 pounds of muscle and a lineman for the New York Giants; *you* tell him Rosey is girlie. (I think it's a fine name.)

Some guys are nicknamed for a particular talent or area of interest. Johnnie "Guitar" Jones can play the blues; Michael "Touchdown" Guilbeault could run with a pigskin. William "Schlitzy" Robinson is about two years older than me, and I think he stole the nickname that—based on my interests as a twenty-something—should have been mine. It may be just as well. *Thoughts of an Average Joe* by Schlitzy Wright doesn't have the same ring to it.

In some families, including mine, a homely name is per-petuated because . . . well, I don't know why. My grandfather was named Rufus Ralph Wright. I'm thinking his father, my great-grandfather, was either mean or just had a twisted sense of humor. (Winnie says I come by it honestly.)

Gramps didn't go by Rufus (imagine that); everyone I knew called him Skip. He was a commanding officer in the army, and Skip was a shortening of Skipper. Still, he felt compelled to pass Rufus Ralph on to my dad; I think he passed along the strange sense of humor, too!

Dad goes, of course, by Jim. My nana didn't want to call him Rufus Jr., or just plain old Junior, so naturally he became Jim. In my sixty-one years, I've never, except for the time Dad bluffed my uncle D.I. out of a $12 pot at the poker table up to deer camp, heard anyone call him anything other than Jim, Dad, or Grampa.

My older brother is Rufus Ralph Wright III. I know . . . why? He goes by Sam. The story I hear is that my folks didn't want to call him Rufus or Ralphie. Again . . . imagine that. Mom and Dad called him "Sandy" when he was a little guy, because of his hair color, and "Sam" became the obvious, more masculine, shortening of "Sandy." Now, it makes sense, right?

Sam has no sons, but has two lovely daughters. I think you'll be relieved to know that neither of my nieces is named Rufus Ralph Wright IV.

Sometimes the Truth Hurts

MY BUDDY J.P., knowing I like to spin a tale, once offered advice for which I've been very grateful. "Never let the truth stand in the way of a good story," he counseled. I've heeded his sage advice on many occasions. I guess you could say I've lied, but I've stretched the truth only in the interest of entertaining others.

Well . . . come to think of it, that's a lie. There may have been other times I've been less than honest, because sometimes *dishonesty* is the best policy.

For instance, I lied for the sake of kindness (and survival) when answering the following questions:

"Sweetheart, do you think that Vanna White is prettier than me?"

"This lasagna is better than your mother's, isn't it?"

"This is my baby girl, Rosie; isn't she cute?"

And most importantly: "Honey, does this dress make me look fat?"

Lying is not a new art form; it's not the invention of some twenty-first-century politician. The importance of honesty has been underscored in our history through the legacies of two of our most popular presidents—the ones for whom we get a Monday off in February—Honest Abe Lincoln and George Washington.

Most Americans are familiar with the story of our first president confessing to his father, "I cannot tell a lie. It was me who chopped down your cherry tree." I have to wonder if his father took him behind the woodshed and gave him a good whoopin', after which young George decided, *The devil with this honesty crap. That didn't work out so well. I think I'll become a politician instead.*

From my own experience, I can tell you that whoever decided "Honesty is the best policy" never, in a moment of guilty conscience, told his mother he'd stolen a Reese's Peanut Butter Cup from Dan's Market. It didn't take me long to realize I shouldn't have burdened my dear mom with that information. It *really* upset her.

Over the years, though, I've found it is best, *in most cases,* to tell the truth. As I mature, I find it increasingly difficult to remember a story if it doesn't represent what actually transpired. It's a lot easier to remember the truth.

My younger brother, K.C., used to drink a lot of beer. As it works out, wobbly pops are not memory enhancers. Consequently, K.C. would frequently run into trouble when trying to come up with a consistent alibi to explain the four hours it took him to make the ten-minute commute from work to home on a Friday night. He'd arrive home at nine o'clock with a story about working overtime and then, in the morning, remind his young wife, Renée, that he'd been late because he'd attended a meeting for volunteer firemen. *Busted!*

It turns out that Renée, or "The Secretary of War," as K.C. calls her (he is smart enough, by the way, to avoid shortening that to the acronym SOW), is bothered significantly more by

K.C.'s lying than by his drinking. My little brother's pretty sharp. It took him only about five years to figure that out.

K.C. still occasionally stops at Luigi's for a beer, or four, on his way home from work. He likes to spend quality time with his buddy, Andy. Of course, K.C. calls Andy "Angelino," because . . . well . . . guys like to make up stupid nicknames for each other.

Following K.C. and Angelino's most recent bonding session, my brother arrived home late and was met at the door by his angry Secretary of War.

"Why are you so late?" she asked.

And then it happened. K.C. answered with, of all things, the truth. "Because I couldn't drink any faster," he replied.

It was on this evening K.C. learned that sometimes the truth hurts, but only for a few minutes. The rolling pin–induced knot on his head was far easier to endure than the usual weekend of quiet, cold suppers and sleeping on the couch.

There's a lot more I could say about the pitfalls of deceit, but I think I'll wrap it up here for fear of being viewed as an expert on the subject.

So, What *Is* Victoria's Secret?

I'M NOT CERTAIN EXACTLY WHEN IT HAPPENED, but I think some-where between the ages of ten and twelve I started noticing there were anatomical differences between me and females of the opposite gender.

During the summer of my twelfth birthday, my mother caught me peeking out my bedroom window at our fifteen-year-old neighbor, Donna, and her friend, Patty, as they sunbathed in their backyard. We didn't know about the sun's damaging effects back then, so I'm sure they had slathered on layers of baby oil to enhance the sun's burning power, thereby destroying another layer of epidermis. I haven't seen either of them for forty years, but I'm guessing these days they're slath-ering on anti-wrinkle creams and having age spots surgically lopped off.

Anyway, they were small girls and they wore two-piece bathing suits, but I'm not sure they'd be considered bikinis. By today's standards, they covered a lot of skin. There was enough material in each to make three to four modern-day swimsuits. Still, my adolescent acts of voyeurism left me with a warm feeling in my belly I didn't understand.

That feeling, of course, disappeared immediately with the sound of my mother's voice. "Joseph Wright, what are you looking at with your daddy's binoculars?"

Oops . . . *Busted.*

Many years later, I guess I still don't understand what that funny feeling is all about, but I do know it has cost me hundreds of thousands of dollars.

Growing up in the North Country, there were lots of reasons to be excited about the impending arrival of spring each year—longer days, warmer temperatures, the melting snow giving way to green grass and budding leaves, and the end of the school year. To a twelve-year-old boy, however, none of those outweighed the vernal appearance of the summer Sears and Roebuck catalog.

Starting on May 1, I'd check the mailbox every day in anticipation of the catalog's arrival. Its pages were packed with photographs of tools, guns, toys, and fishing gear. But, to be honest, back then, it was the softer side of Sears that piqued my interest. There must have been thirty pages of women modeling underwear, bathing suits, and lingerie. Thinking back, it was mostly older women in granny undies and industrial-strength brassieres, but I didn't care. It was women in underwear, and I was twelve.

When I was a little older, I found a copy of one of Hugh Hefner's magazines in the sandpaper drawer of my uncle Jack's workshop. I spent a lot of time woodworking that summer. Mom was pleased that I'd taken such an interest in carpentry. I think Dad knew better.

A few years ago when my son Jake was sixteen, I noticed he'd taken great interest in the incoming postal deliveries. He was checking the mailbox three times a day. I figured, for sure, he was anxiously awaiting the delivery of the latest Sears catalog, and thought it must have finally arrived the first week in April, because from April 3 to April 9 he left his room only to eat and use the bathroom. April 10 was a school day, so I did some investigating while the kids were in classes.

I searched Jake's room for nearly an hour before I discovered a hidden treasure in his sock drawer. It was a catalog called *Victoria's Secret*, and I wasn't sure my boy should be looking at it, so I studied it . . . for three hours. I couldn't believe what I was seeing on those glossy, full-color pages. These were the most beautiful women I'd ever laid eyes on! They were nothing like the everyday women I'd admired in the Sears catalogs, and the articles of underwear they modeled were much more attractive (and revealing) than the full-torso, body-armor girdles of those 1960s advertisements. This was like free porn!

I think I was stuck on page fifty-six when the little woman barged into Jake's room and caught me, catalog in hand, pupils dilated, trying to figure out *Victoria's Secret*.

"What have you been doing in here for three hours?" she asked. Then she spotted my reading material and I knew I was in trouble.

"Why, you old pervert. These women aren't even real, you know." Her face was turning red and her eyes were wide. It was a look I've learned to fear. "They've all been surgically enhanced, and they use that Photoshop to airbrush out any defects in their bodies."

I tried to think fast, but a lot of blood had flowed away from my cerebrum, so I just blurted out the first words that passed through my limited gray matter.

"Who cares why they look good? I'm a full-grown man, and I'll look at any pictures I want to. And if you don't like it, take a hike."

I told her who was boss. I didn't see Winnie for about a week. On the eighth day, I was able to open my right eye a little bit.

Weird Dreams

MY DREAMS SCARE ME SOMETIMES. It's not that they are frightening in a Freddy Krueger, horror-movie kind of way. It's just that they make no sense—at least not to me.

Last week, I dreamt of being chased down the street where I lived as a kid by a 1968 VW bus with peace symbols and flowers painted on its exterior. Instead of wheels, the bus had a hundred centipede legs and, where the grille and headlights belonged, was the face of my third-grade teacher, Mrs. Wilson. I haven't thought about my third-grade teacher (or her support hose–covered ankles) since I was in fourth grade, about a hundred years ago. So why is her face chasing me while I sleep? And why was that many-legged VW bus able to move so quickly while my legs were performing as if I was knee-deep in quicksand?

I made the mistake of posing that very question to my buddy, Thurm Seigars, whose tofu-loving, transcendental-meditating wife, Moonbeam, is a self-proclaimed expert dream analyst.

Thurm couldn't wait to deliver my diagnosis. "Moonbeam says you have some unresolved issue with your third-grade teacher, which makes you invite conflict and fear into your life. You are running from peace."

"Well, tell Moonbeam she's full of horse-puckey!" I said. "I ate three black-bean burritos and a side of jalapeño poppers that night. That's the explanation for my crazy dream."

Why do scary, weird dreams recur while more pleasant dreams disappear for good as soon as I wake from them? Like when my dream involves two bikini-clad Patriots cheerleaders, me, and a hot tub full of warm Mazola oil, I can't fall back to sleep fast enough, hoping to see how it turns out. (It never happens.)

The centipede-legged, Mrs. Wilson–faced peace bus, however, continues to chase me without fail as soon as I drift off.

Life just isn't fair.

You Don't Tug on Superman's Cape

SOME LIFE DECISIONS ARE DIFFICULT. Lately, I've been struggling over whether to travel in my gas-guzzling Dodge half-
ton or a tiny Japanese hybrid pickup truck. Sure, I'd like to
save some money on gasoline and reduce my carbon footprint,
but what if the little truck won't haul the massive buck I'm
likely to bag this fall?

And then there's the age-old question: Should I go on
a diet? Sure, I'm heavier than I ought to be, but will losing
twenty pounds really change my love life or enhance my
chances for a career in modeling? It seems unlikely. And
besides, I'd have to replace my wardrobe and drink that sixty-
four-calorie beer/water.

On the other hand, some decisions should be no-brainers.
Apparently, these require at least a pea-size brain, because
many people seem incapable of choosing wisely. Jim Croce
summarized a few decisions that should require little, if any,
thought when he sang: "You don't tug on Superman's cape;
you don't spit into the wind; you don't pull the mask off an
old Lone Ranger . . ."

I might add to this list of seemingly obvious choices. You
don't pee on an electric fence . . . it's shocking. Especially to
the poor individual who hears the girlish scream and then
finds the outdoor urinater dazed, wet, grinning, and giggling
like Crazy Ernie at the Smalltown Fourth of July fireworks

display. They tell me I recovered from the electrocution within twelve hours.

Last June, my father was fly-fishing on the Moose River when a flatlander walked up alongside him and started casting into the hole Dad had been working for twenty minutes. That was a poor decision—unthinkable, really. It's worse than tapping the groom on the shoulder to "cut in" during a couple's first dance as husband and wife—you just don't do it. I wonder if, while the emergency room doctor extracted a Warden's Worry dry fly from his left earlobe, the flatlander reconsidered his decision to share Dad's fishing hole.

Sometimes, poor decisions are accidental. That was certainly the case when a certain author/outdoorsman chose to sit on a rock near a deer run practically in the shadow of my brother-in-law's tree stand. I was wandering aimlessly through a hardwood stand one November when I stumbled upon what appeared to be an excellent place to wait for a buck to walk by. My brother-in-law Jimbo couldn't have agreed more. He'd scouted these woods diligently all October, and had chosen this spot to set up his tree stand because of the heavy traffic on the deer runs which lead from the thick cover of the softwood swamp to the beechnuts up the ridge, upon which the deer had been feeding. He'd logged in thirty or more long, cold hours in this spot during the previous four days without seeing a deer, but he knew what his game camera had captured in October, and was determined to be patient.

Needless to say, he was less than pleased to see me stumble up the ridge, seemingly breaking every branch in my path, only to plop my backside on a rock not fifty yards down the hill from his carefully placed stand. I'm sorry I didn't see him. Maybe I would have if he hadn't spent so much time building a camouflage blind around his tree stand. He says I should have smelled his fox urine scent cover. I guess the aroma of my canned, smoked herring covered his cover. And how was I supposed to hear his whistling over the crackling of my Snickers bar wrappers?

Jimbo was really upset with me—so angry, in fact, that he didn't even help me drag that eight-point, 220-pound buck out of the woods.

I've Noticed that Women Are Not like Men

OH SURE, I NOTICED the obvious physical differences between the genders at an early age. By about twelve years old, that observation was nearing obsession. But recently, after thirty-some years of living with a female, I'm catching on that there are some other significant differences as well.

I've noticed women, especially mothers, worry more and sleep less than I do. Our beautiful daughter Maggie lives in a big city several hours away from Smalltown, and if she calls while the little woman is away and I speak to her, the post-call debriefing goes something like this:

"Did she say what she's doing this weekend?" Winnie will ask.

"No," I'll reply.

"Was she at work when she called?"

"Yup."

"When was she going home?"

"She didn't say," I'll answer.

"Is she taking a cab or the subway home?"

"I don't know."

"Jeez, Joe, you never ask the right questions," the little woman will growl.

"Well, jeez, Winnie, she's thirty years old. She can think for herself."

"Oh, you just don't get it!" Winnie will respond, rolling her eyes.

"Nope, I don't."

Winnie tells me she sleeps only three to four hours a night. She says it's because of hormones and worrying about the kids. It seems to annoy her that I sometimes toss and turn for two to three minutes before I can nod off for the night.

Women seem to care more about appearances than men do. I've noticed that when I take Winnie over to the Smalltown Congregational Church bean supper, she gets all dolled up in her best sweat suit with the matching top and bottom, but I wear the same jeans and mustard-stained flannel shirt I wore to dig up the septic-tank cover earlier that day.

The little woman also insists that I keep the various rusted body parts of my soon-to-be-restored (I've been saying this for ten years now) 1943 Dodge pickup truck in the backyard, instead of beside the garage where I can get at them. Maybe she's afraid that someone will spot it and want to buy it if it's visible from the street.

The ladies don't seem to appreciate the fun things in life, like sitting outside at minus-10 degrees Fahrenheit and waiting for a deer to walk by or an ice-fishing flag to pop up.

I've also learned (sometimes the hard way) that women are more thin-skinned than men. I can call my buddy Roy "a fat, smelly, egg-sucking warthog," and it's taken as a term of endearment. However, if I would greet Roy's wife with "Mimi, you sweaty, old, bloated, manure-covered heifer," my little woman would become an instant widow, and you'd be reading about the homicide in the *Smalltown News*.

Things I Shouldn't Have Said

As I may have already mentioned, I seem to be missing that brain-to-tongue filter that would save me from saying the kinds of things that can lead to a serious butt-whoopin' by an angry husband, or the wrath of Winnie, the little woman.

I'll admit that not all of my stories are totally true, but this one is . . . I swear it.

My buddies Munzie, Barney, Walt, and Warren and I were at the Oxford County Bluegrass Festival, and we'd been playing music outside Walt's motor home for most of the weekend. We had all noticed a couple in their mid-fifties who'd spent a lot of time standing and listening to our songs. We were all curious about who they were. Munzie figured they were talent scouts from Nashville who were mightily impressed with his guitar and vocal virtuosity, and were waiting for the right moment to offer him a big recording contract. The rest of us were figuring them to be either hearing-impaired or just easily entertained.

By late Saturday night, curiosity (and Jim Beam) had gotten the best of me. We finished a rousing rendition of "The Ballad of Jed Clampett," and I couldn't help myself. I turned to our new fans and asked the powerfully built giant of a man standing there with his lovely wife, "So, who are you, anyway?"

"I'm Rob Mason," he politely answered.

"Mason? Mason?" I repeated. "I shoulda known you were a mason. Your wife's built like a brick outhouse."

There was a moment of silence and, for a minute, I felt as though I was in a vacuum caused by the collective gasps of my friends who, by now, feared for my life. Fortunately, Mr. and Mrs. Mason were not thin-skinned and accepted my awkward "I meant it as a compliment" apology.

I'm not a mean person, honestly. I'm just sometimes misunderstood . . . or stupid.

I meant well when I said, "Honey, I like the way that dress fits you now; it's a lot tighter than it used to be," and when the little woman complained of being tired after stacking two cords of firewood, while I watched the Patriots lose to the Colts, I reassured her that her fatigue was to be expected, because, "You're not as young as you used to be." I thought I was being sensitive. She didn't take it that way.

My daughter Maggie's friend, Hannah, won't have much to do with me these days. I guess I said something to upset her. It was just another misunderstanding. You see, I hadn't seen Hannah for nearly a year when I ran into her in the potato chip aisle at Dan's Market. My end of the conversation went something like this.

"Hey, Hannah! You're looking great! Congratulations! When are you due? . . . Oh, you're not? . . . Well, umm . . . sorry."

My buddy Munzie seems to have the same brain-to-tongue-filter deficiency as me, especially when it comes to talking to my wife, Winnie. His greatest offense occurred as he was trying to describe his latest female object of interest. "Wanda is small and tiny the way I like my women," Munzie explained to Winnie. "I like 'em even smaller than you."

Oh, boy, I said to myself. *This isn't going to go well.*

You see, Winnie isn't very big, and she's a good-looking woman. I'm pretty sure Munzie, in his awkward way, was trying to pay the little woman a compliment. It just wasn't working.

"She's some pretty too," he explained. "Compared to her, even you are a dog." (Again, a clumsy compliment.) "But she's quite a bit younger than you."

Winnie had heard enough, and commenced to read Munzie the riot act for several minutes, concluding with, "Munzie, you pea-brained doofus! You just called me old, fat, and ugly within a five-minute span."

Munzie's defense? "I never said you was old."

Barbie Jennings was the sexiest girl in my class at Small-town High. I saw her at our thirtieth class reunion and met her new husband, Irv, a seemingly mild-mannered certified public accountant. Irv seemed a bit uncomfortable, standing alone near the bar as his wife flitted about the room, reacquainting herself with her old friends. I felt bad for him, so I thought I'd do what I could to make him feel at ease.

"You're a lucky man, Irv," I said. "You should have seen Barbie back in high school. She was *really* good-looking back then . . . she had *lots* of boyfriends. I think half the guys in our class went out with her . . . and she was *lots* of fun. And I mean *lots of fun,* if you know what I mean, Irv. You must be quite a man, to keep up with her in the old boudoir, huh, Irv?"

I winked at him and ducked just in time to avoid his left hook. Some folks just can't take a compliment.

My Duct-Tape Darlin'

As I've mentioned before, I play in a band called Basic Bluegrass with my buddies Roy, Munzie, Walt, Barney, and Warren. Walt's a builder, and one night, following a practice session at his place, Munzie noticed that Walt had some trim lumber duct-taped to the rack on his pickup truck.

"Ahh, good ol' duct tape," Munzie said. "There ain't much you can't do with duct tape. Jeez, Joe, you should write a song about that."

And so "My Duct-Tape Darlin'," a tender love ballad, was born. Since duct tape is such an important component of life—especially Smalltown life—I thought I'd share with you the lyrics of "My Duct-Tape Darlin'," along with a brief history of the song's evolution.

I had myself a pretty girl, but she was from the South—
I made her darn near perfect with duct tape across her mouth.
I taped her to the bedpost to be sure that she would stay,
But a man came selling Ginsu knives and took my girl away.

Chorus: *(repeat after each verse)*
You can use it on the homestead, on the car or on the farm,
You can even use that duct tape to fix your broken arm.
You can patch up your Toyota before it falls apart,
But all the duct tape in this world won't fix my broken heart.

That girl went off and left me, and I haven't seen her since;
She ran off with that salesman who thought he was her prince.
They found him in Miami, fastened to the throne.
(It seems my little darlin' had some duct tape of her own.)

If you should find a sweetheart, I'll give you some advice:
If you want to keep her quiet, wrap the duct tape twice.
And if you can't be certain that woman will be true,
Strap her to the bedpost with duct tape and Super Glue.

So, those were the original lyrics to my beautiful love ballad. Kinda brings a tear to your eye, doesn't it? We've performed this song for fifteen years or so now, and it has evolved into a fan favorite. Our fans seem to like the more stupid stuff.

After thousands (all right, maybe a hundred) performances of this song, we started to get a little tired of it, so every few years, I've added a verse to spice it up a bit. The added lines have been based on events in the news; as such, "My Duct-Tape Darlin' " has become a tender love ballad with political overtones.

The Bill Clinton verse:

There's a big old office in a house that's painted white;
Bill should have a lid on what goes on there day and night.
A little roll of duct tape might have helped out quite a bit
To quiet down dear Monica, and even Linda Tripp.

Thoughts of an Average Joe

After the tragedy of September 11, 2001, I felt I should write a verse about Osama bin Laden. I'd heard he liked horses and donkeys, but I don't like to use the same word twice in a verse if I can help it, so I searched for another word for *donkey*. I searched the dictionary, the thesaurus, and even the Bible, and finally, I found that word. The Osama bin Laden verse became prophetic, although it took years longer than any of us imagined or hoped it would.

> *Osama bin Laden, we know that you're a fool*
> *We hear that you like horses, and you've got a donkey, too.*
> *With a little roll of duct tape, keep that donkey by your side*
> *And that way when we find you, you can kiss your ass good-bye.*

In February 2006, Vice President Dick Cheney shot a hunting partner, apparently mistaking him for a quail. I wrote another verse:

> *Vice President Cheney, he really likes to hunt*
> *He uses camo duct tape to camouflage his gun.*
> *He only shot a lawyer, so he didn't get a fine*
> *Maybe he'd consider taking Hillary next time!*

As you might imagine, the royalties from my songs are just pouring in. In fact, I just cashed a Broadcast Music, Inc. check and bought a brand-new truck . . . a Tonka for my grandson, Hanson.

Part VI: Things that Annoy Me

I'm Not Ready for the Wireless World

I'M ONE OF THOSE DINOSAURS who still has a telephone attached to my wall, and to the rest of the world, with wires. That's because the part of the country in which the little woman and I live isn't ready to be part of the "wireless world." Most of my friends have gone cellular, which is why I have had to learn a new language, sort of like Pig Latin (ig-Pay atin-Lay). These days, I have to figure out the other end of a conversation while hearing only two out of every three or four words. I'm telling you, sometimes it's very difficult—even dangerous—to respond.

How do I answer my wife's friend, Sandra, when the question sounds like this? "I'd like *blip* have you *blip blip* over and maybe show *blip blip blip* and maybe *blip blip* breasts. Would you *blip blip blip* interested?"

"Umm . . . well . . . I'm sorry, Sandra, could you say that again?"

My face turned red the other day while I was standing in the checkout line at Dan's Market. I was in front of my buddy Roy's son, Coleman, who had never had a lot to say to me.

"Hi, how ya doin'?" he asks.

"Good," I reply. "You?"

"I'm good. Just got outta work. Stopped by Dan's to pick up a twelve-pack," he says.

"I see that," I reply. "So, how's the old man? I haven't seen him this week."

Coleman looks at me funny, but keeps the conversation flowing. I'm quite flattered actually.

"Hey man, wanna come over and catch the Sox game tonight? Maybe pound back a few cold ones?"

Now I'm really flabbergasted. "Oh, thanks, Cole. I appreciate the offer, but I promised the little woman I'd take her to the bean supper down to the church tonight."

Coleman just shakes his head and says, "Hey man, I gotta hang up. One of my dad's old buddies is standing next to me and keeps answering my questions." He touches that Green Tooth, or whatever it's called, in his left ear and slaps me on the back.

"Hi, Joe, how ya doin'?"

I try to act as cool as possible and reply, "Oh, hi, Cole; I didn't notice you standing behind me."

Dropped calls are particularly annoying. I hate it when I rattle off a most charming and hilarious story for two to three minutes, nail the punch line, and then listen for the response . . . Silence. Now that's particularly tough for me because, about half the time, silence is the response to my hilarious anecdotes even without a dropped call. But when I realize I've been talking to myself for who knows how long, it really aggravates me. To make things worse, I'm suspicious that some of my friends have mastered the dropped-call fake, and will use it at my very mention of a funny story.

If World War II made my parents part of the Greatest Generation, then cellular technology has turned Generation Y into the Rudest Generation. They don't seem to recognize that texting, tweeting, and answering their cell phones five times during a ten-minute face-to-face conversation with me could make a guy feel his company is unappreciated and his words unimportant. God forbid they should miss a message on that little electronic gizmo. Makes me want to break their nimble little thumbs.

Call me an old-fashioned, backward-thinking, narrow-minded old fool if you want to. Just don't call me on your cell phone.

Be Careful What You Say

I'M NOT ALL THAT BRIGHT, but I'm kind of a word nerd. I'm easily (and probably inappropriately) annoyed by the misuse of language. You can cheat me, lie to me, even cut me off on the highway, and I'll let it slide. But a hanging preposition at the end of your sentence is like fingernails on a chalkboard to me.

Last Tuesday, Merlin Remington, my supervisor at work, handed me the company's eighty-page employee policy manual and said, "Joe, please peruse this at your leisure, when you get a minute, and then return it to me."

"Okay, Merlin," I replied. "You're the boss. I'll peruse the manual if you'd like, but it'll take me all day. Don't you have something else for me to do today?"

Merlin's eyes widened and I could measure his pulse by watching the blood flow through the dilated arteries at his temples. I knew I had him.

"Don't give me that crap, Joe. Just quickly peruse the manual, initial the last page, and return it to me."

"You're confusing me, Merlin. How can I quickly study the manual in great detail?" I asked.

Merlin's forehead furrowed. "Don't study it, Joe. Peruse it."

"But, to peruse is to study in great detail. Check out *Webster's Dictionary*."

A lot of folks overuse and misuse the word *literally*. There's a commercial running on TV right now in which one of the actors says, "The savings were so amazing, I literally fell out of my chair!" Oh, come on; does she expect me to believe she was so excited she keeled over and landed on her back on the linoleum, legs and arms pointing toward heaven, spastically flailing about? I doubt that.

I hadn't seen my cousin Ernie since we were in college, where I introduced him to his lovely wife, Melinda, who was one of the prettiest girls at Smalltown State. I can't imagine what she saw in Ernie. Anyway, during a recent conversation, he told me they have a beautiful, blonde-haired, blue-eyed, five-year-old granddaughter, Emily, who is the "spitting image" of Melinda. I'm not sure how to take that. Does Ernie mean that sweet little Emily looks like her grandmother only when she spits? Does she spit a lot? Does Melinda spit a lot now? Do they both chew Red Man or Copenhagen and carry a paper spit cup?

I suspected Ernie meant to say that Emily is the "spit *and* image" of her lovely grandmother; at least, I hope so.

Finally, the grammar misuse, which I'm sure goes unnoticed by normal people, but drives me crazy, is the misplacement of the word *only* in a sentence. I hear it every day, even from the mouths of learned broadcast analysts and political pundits.

I'm sure lyricist Al Dubin was trying to pay the ultimate compliment to the object of his classic song, "I Only Have Eyes for You." But did he actually mean he liked only the way his lover looked; that her voice made his skin crawl; or that he found her personality exceedingly annoying? I doubt it. I suspect he meant, "I Have Eyes Only for You." I guess that doesn't sound as good, and he should be allowed to play the poetic-license card, but it still annoys me.

What if I told you I only go to church on Sundays? Would you believe I spend all day at prayer service and never watch football, drink beer, fish, or play poker on Sundays? No, the truth is I go to church only on Sundays . . . hardly ever on a Wednesday.

No New Year's Resolutions for Me

I DON'T MAKE NEW YEAR'S RESOLUTIONS. I know I won't keep them anyway, so why bother? I do make a "New Week's" resolution every Monday morning—to lose weight! It typically lasts until about suppertime.

I'm overweight . . . kinda fat. I like food, and not just any food; I like the bad stuff—potato chips, pie, chocolate, burgers, fries. . . . I like the stuff that's supposed to be good for me too—salad, vegetables, fruit, rice . . . The problem is that I like everything, and lots of it.

To make things worse, the little woman, Winnie, eats like a bird, and—get this—she hates chocolate and ice cream and cake and donuts—anything sweet, really. I'm not saying she can take it or leave it; she really *hates* it. That's just wrong, isn't it? All I can figure is that her DNA must be screwed up. There must be a misplaced sweet-tooth chromosome somewhere along her double helix that distorts her sense of good vs. bad, tasty vs. repulsive. I fear I may have done irreparable damage to our species by giving in to her tireless pleas to help her reproduce. Okay, I was the one begging, but I'm just saying, I feel a little bad about enabling the propagation of this defective trait to another generation.

It's really not all my fault that I'm fat. Let's face it: There are lots of opportunities to take in calories out there, and I can resist anything . . . except temptation.

There's even temptation at work. As I've mentioned, my coworker Candi is a baking diva—the queen of tarts. Every Monday and Wednesday, she arrives at the office with a chocolate raspberry torte, cinnamon sticky buns, or some other equally delicious and decadent treat. I *could* choose not to eat her offerings, but I don't. I really like them, and it shows. Candi, on the other hand, is a physical fitness nut who obviously hasn't enjoyed a cookie or brownie in years. She's probably too stuffed after the sixteen peas and two teaspoons of cheese curds she scarfs down at lunch every day.

I've decided I have a couple of choices: I can limit my intake to spinach, rice cakes, dried-out chicken, and tofu; or I can just hang out with people fatter than me. I choose the latter option.

So these days, I spend a lot of time at bluegrass festivals, county fairs, and Small-Mart. It makes me feel better about myself, and besides, fat folks are more fun than skinny people.

You have to be industrious, determined, disciplined, and a bit neurotic—maybe even obsessive-compulsive—to be thin. Does that sound like the kind of person you want to party with?

I've heard of folks described as "fat and happy," but I've never heard of anyone being described as "thin and happy." I suspect there's a reason for that. When you picture a jolly person, does a stick-thin supermodel come to mind? I didn't think so.

I did just read about a study that claimed thin people live longer, but I'm wondering . . . does it just *seem* longer?

I won't be making a New Year's resolution this year—but if I did, it would be to eat every day as if it was the last day of my life.

Fly the Friendly Skies

GROWING UP IN SMALLTOWN, I didn't know many people from outside our county, so I didn't fly in an airplane until my brother Sam went to Fort Lauderdale for spring break and my father and I had to fly down there to bail him out of jail. (It seems that in those days, mooning a police officer from a moving vehicle was frowned upon.)

Anyway, traveling by air then was much simpler than it is now. We drove to Manchester to board a plane and got off in Miami. No lines, no waits, no hassles. My, how things have changed, thanks to Osama bin Laden and his Koran-thumping jihadists. These days, traveling by air is a whole lot different, and a big inconvenience.

About a year ago, my brother-in-law Rick, a dairy farmer, wanted to go to the Northeastern Holstein Heifer Breeding and Farm Equipment Show down in Pennsylvania, and since he can't afford to leave his cows for long, we decided to fly. I'm not sure why he invited me to join him, because I don't know squat about manure spreaders and could care less about teat symmetry or any other quality that makes a good heifer good. Besides, all I could think about was how far we'd sunk from road trips to Sherbrooke, Quebec, thirty years ago, when our only mission was to check out a whole different breed of heifers—young, Canadian heifers. (I must admit, though, we were judging them accordingly for some of the same physical attributes.)

Being tied to the farm and all, Rick doesn't get out into the real world much. This was his first exposure to the employees of the Transportation Security Administration. He seemed less than impressed by the caliber of talent charged with protecting our national security. Rick is a very bright person. He's also like his sister, Winnie, my darling wife, in another, sometimes frightening way. He lets folks know what he's thinking; he doesn't pull any punches. He calls a spade a spade. That didn't work out so well during our encounter with the TSA.

We arrived down to the airport in Manchester by 6:00 a.m. for our 8:15 a.m. flight to Philadelphia.

"Why in God's name did we need to get here so early?" Rick sputtered as he grabbed his Dan's Market plastic grocery-bag luggage from the backseat of my pickup truck.

"You'll see," I explained. "It's all about safety."

About then, we arrived at the security check-in where there was a long, serpentine line with at least a hundred people between us and the TSA agent.

"Get in line, Rick," I said.

"I ain't gettin' in that foolish line," he grumbled.

"If you want to fly to Philly, you are."

"Well, jumpin' jeezum, if this ain't the stupidest thing I've ever seen. Do I look like a damned terrorist to you, Joe?"

"Shhh . . . it's for our own safety, Rick. Now, be careful what you say here."

"Careful, my keister," he says. "I think these folks need some guidance."

Oh, jeez, I thought. I could tell this wasn't going to go well.

After a half-hour of shuffling along the snaking line and thirty announcements about liquids, firearms, fireworks, and explosives, Rick made it to the chubby, bald, Latino TSA agent named Juan who wore thick, brown, plastic-framed eyeglasses. That's when the trouble really started.

Rick handed the man his boarding pass and photo ID.

"Where are you traveling to, sir?" Juan asked.

"I'm going to Philadelphia, just like it says in plain English on that piece of paper I just handed ya. You *can* read, can't ya?"

The agent glared over his spectacles. "Yes, Mr. London, I can read. We just have to check."

"Well, that's stupid," Rick explained.

"Sir, please place your luggage, jacket, belt, shoes, and any metal objects in these trays and place them on the conveyor."

"My shoes? What kind of idiot puts a bomb in his shoes?"

"Richard Reid, alias Abdel Rahim—al-Qaeda."

Rick threw his size elevens into the tray. "Well, you can at least speak English. You're in America now, boy."

"Sir, do you have any explosives, firearms, or fireworks in your possession?" Juan asked.

"Are you kidding me? What kind of a bonehead question is that?" Rick asked. "Sure, I'm carrying a Colt .45 and a pocketful of M-80s."

Juan motioned for a really big Asian man, built like a Sumo wrestler. Hideki pulled my brother-in-law aside and explained the pat-down procedure to him.

"Oh, come on," Rick complained. "Why are you picking on me?"

"We're not picking on you, sir. We randomly check a passenger from time to time. It's for your own safety and that of your fellow passengers."

Hideki started the pat-down and, when he reached a sensitive area, Rick flinched and said, "You'd better not touch me like that again, Hideki, unless you give me a big diamond ring first."

"Sorry, sir. It's procedure. I have to be sure you aren't hiding a firearm or explosives."

Rick rolled his eyes. "Well, you'd better check, then, 'cause I'm hiding gunpowder in my crotch and I'm packin' a dynamite suppository."

"Sir, I wish you hadn't said that."

I'm not sure how many agents it took to restrain Rick for the cavity search, but I'm guessing it was several. Meanwhile, there was trouble with Rick's luggage screening.

"Mr. London, inside one of your grocery bags we found a small Styrofoam cooler which held one container of liquid."

"That's not liquid," Rick explained. "That's semen."

"Excuse me?"

"It's semen in that container."

"Umm, sir, *whose* semen?"

"That's my semen," Rick declared.

"Your semen? Sir, there's eight ounces there."

"Well, it belongs to me. It's actually Hercules' semen. What do you think—I'm some kind of pervert?"

"Hercules, sir? Really?"

"Yeah, my bull, Hercules. I'm takin' his semen to Pennsylvania to find him a worthy heifer."

"Well, Mr. London, if you're going to make that happen for Hercules, you're going to have to check the bag."

Rick threw his arms in the air as a gesture of relief. "If by bag, you mean udder, then you are finally getting your thick head around the purpose of this godforsaken trip."

So, long story short (too late for that), we made it to the Northeastern Holstein Heifer Breeding and Farm Equipment Show in Pennsylvania. A heifer was found for Hercules, and my brother-in-law was interrogated, scanned, fondled, poked, and, on the return trip . . . very cooperative.

I'm Not Ready for a Paperless World

I LOVE BOOKS AND NEWSPAPERS, and even a good magazine once in a while. It's not just the reading I enjoy. I love the sound a new book makes when you crack its binding for the first time, and the smell of new ink on newspaper. I love the musty essence of an old book; it makes me wonder where it has been, whose hands have held it, and who has flipped its pages over the years. When I imagine an old book's previous readers, it is always the image of an ancient scholar or regal sea captain that fills my mind. Never do I picture a coughing, sneezing, phlegm-producing plague victim sitting on a bedpan with his or her hands on my old novel.

The little woman and I have hundreds, maybe thousands, of books we can't bring ourselves to get rid of. Though we realize that most of them will never be read again, it's fun to look at them from time to time. They remind me of whatever was going on in my life at the time I read a particular book, or even how that book might have changed the way I think about life. Seeing my old copy of *A Tale of Two Cities* conjures up images of Stinky Bean puking into a flowerpot at Mitch Norway's parents' camp. (Mitch threw a keg party the night after my English IV final exam.)

I'm concerned that more and more, people are getting their news from the computer or TV, instead of through the local newspaper. People are even downloading novels onto their laptops or Kindle readers and reading them on their electronic devices. I don't get it. It's just not the same as holding a book, newspaper, or magazine in your hands and turning the pages.

What if books and newspapers go away completely? I do some of my best reading while I'm sitting on the throne. I can't imagine spending that special part of my day with a computer on my lap; that just wouldn't be right.

I have fond memories of my early years as a newspaper delivery boy, when I would take my forty-three copies of the *Smalltown News* and deliver them to my customers. It was my first venture into the business world, and I learned a lot.

I learned that providing good service would earn me tips, cookies, or brownies. I learned that it felt good to earn my own money, which I could spend on myself or use to buy Christmas presents for Mom and Dad. I figured out that, to some of my elderly customers, I was more than just the paper-boy. On most days, my daily visit was their only contact with another human being.

I also learned how to survive the attacks of Mr. Labor's German shepherd. Saurkraut was huge, and had a loud bark and big teeth. He was allowed to run free and, apparently, one of his missions in life was to scare the snot out of the paperboy. (He was very good at it.) After several weeks of Saurkraut's attacks, which Mr. Labor seemed to enjoy far too much, I came up with a survival plan.

It seems Saurkraut was easily distracted from his daily attempt to cause me to lose control of my bowels. All it took was a chocolate-flavored "treat" tossed as far as my twelve-year-old arm could throw. After a week of these treats, Mr. Labor kept Saurkraut chained to the garage, apparently in an attempt to control his dog's diet and bowel control. Who knew that chocolate-flavored laxatives could have such an effect on a dog's behavior?

So what if newspapers were to go away? How would kids learn the lessons I learned as a paperboy . . . and what would we use to get the woodstove or campfire burning? Sure, you could potentially read this fascinating, thought-provoking book on your Kindle, but then what would you use to fill up all those bookshelves?

Some Christmas Carols Annoy Me

CHRISTMAS CAROLS SHOULDN'T ANNOY ME, but some of them do. I think a big part of the problem is that radio stations start playing them just after Halloween. By Thanksgiving I'm already tired of hearing Christmas music.

"Let It Snow" must have been written by a real loser. This guy is at his girlfriend's home, *the lights are turned way down low*, and there's a romantic fire in the fireplace. Meanwhile, there's a blizzard outside and the snow *doesn't show signs of stopping*, and this guy's excited because he's *brought some corn for popping*. Is this guy for real? Does he really think that popcorn is going to do what wine, champagne, and tequila have always accomplished so effectively?

He eventually resigns himself to the fact that popcorn isn't going to get the job done, and decides to trudge home through what is by then a foot and a half of snow, proclaiming *if you'll only hold me tight, all the way home I'll be warm.* How pathetic is that? Next time maybe he'll realize that if he takes Jose Cuervo instead of Orville Redenbacher, he'll at the very least be invited to spend the night on the sofa.

I'm not a big fan of "Deck the Halls" either. There are too many fa-la-la-la-la's in that song. And then there's that line: *Don we now our gay apparel*, which seems to be telling me that, through the holiday season, I should pack away my Carhartt overalls, steel-toed boots, and hard hat in favor of leather pants, shiny penny loafers, and a beret. (That would make for some long days at the worksite.)

"Walking in a Winter Wonderland" doesn't make a lot of sense to me. In this song, a young couple decides to build a snowman *and pretend that he is Parson Brown. He'll say, Are you married? We'll say No, man—but you can do the job while you're in town.* It sounds to me as though these two lovebirds hadn't even considered marriage until the snowman minister asked if they were hitched, but then decided, "Hey, now *that's* an idea. Heck, yeah, Parson, since you're in town, we may as well do that. Sounds like fun!"

And then there's "Auld Lang Syne." *Should auld acquaintance be forgot, and never brought to mind?* Most of us have sung these words many times on New Year's Eve, and take the few words of this song that we actually know to mean that we should forget about our old friends and trade them in for some new ones. It's a new year—time to move on. Sure, my old buddy Roy took the rap for me in high school when I painted the school mascot—a live Holstein—pink, so that I wouldn't be kicked off the football team. And it's true that he saved my life in the fight that ensued after I came on to the girlfriend of a giant with GODZILLA embroidered on his black leather Harley-Davidson jacket. So what? He was in the hospital for only a few months. That was in the past. Roy limps only a little now, and it's a new year; time to kick Roy to the curb and find some new friends.

There are a few holiday songs that I *do* like. "Grandma Got Run Over by a Reindeer" is one of them.

Some Folks Shouldn't Wear Spandex

There ought to be a law regulating who can wear spandex or Lycra or, for that matter, bikinis, Speedos, crop-tops, or short-shorts of any material. Heavy people shouldn't be allowed to wear that stuff. If you don't weigh at least twenty-five pounds less than I do (forty pounds for you, ladies), you shouldn't be parading yourself around in a pair of those stretchy bicycling shorts. It ain't pretty, and it ain't appreciated.

You could incite a small earthquake, caused by the collective full-body shivers of those you pass on the street. I know, some of you will insist that you need those biker shorts for the padding they provide to soften your ride. Well, please, just Velcro some foam rubber into a pair of baggy shorts and call it good. You're obviously not competing in marathons anyway. You can make it down to Dunkin' Donuts and back without those special shorts.

I can't imagine what possesses heavy folks to wear clothing that is too tight, too skimpy, or too revealing. All I can figure is they either don't own any mirrors, or they have really messed-up eyesight. Otherwise, no one would leave home looking like so many people I see at the Smalltown Small-Mart or Old Orchard Beach.

Last year, the little woman gave me a three-month membership to the Smalltown House of Fitness where she's been a member for years. She said she thought it would give me something to do during the long winter months. The truth is, she thinks I'm too fat.

On our first visit to the gym, I wore my baggy cotton sweatpants and a Cabela's sweatshirt. Winnie wore a similar outfit. Angie, the cute, little twenty-two-year-old aerobics instructor, wore a tight, bright pink, stretchy workout outfit and looked good in it.

At our second session, Monique Belanger, a mean-spirited busybody, wore the same outfit as Angie. Let me go on record as saying that Monique is twice the woman Angie is . . . in both age and body mass. She apparently has a gift for seeing the worst in others and a self-image so distorted that she sees herself looking like Wonder Woman in an outfit that, in fact, makes her resemble the Michelin Man.

So, like I said, there ought to be a law: To buy certain apparel items you should have to show an ID. If you're over forty, no spandex, Lycra, crop-tops, or short-shorts for you. If you are under forty, you step on one of those new scales that send electronic waves up through your body to deter-mine your BFI (body fat index). If you're over the limit, do the world a favor and go back and trade in the spandex stretch pants for a loose-fitting cotton workout outfit. And no crop-tops either. I don't care who you are, I don't want to see your muffin top hanging out over your undersized jeans. (That goes for you girls, too!)

And fellas, I don't care if the mercury is about to blow the top off the thermometer; if you're not in a whole lot better shape than I am, for crying out loud, keep your shirt on! You could be harpooned at the beach.

Don't get me wrong—I've got nothing against oversized people. Heck, I'm one of 'em! Just do us all a favor: If you have a lot of junk in the trunk, hide it; it's not a treasure to be shared with others.

I Might Need That Someday

I'VE GOT AN ATTIC, A GARAGE, A WORKSHOP, AND A BARN full of stuff that I can't bear to let go. There are tools in my wood-working shop I haven't used in twenty-eight years, but I might need that old wooden miter box someday. Oh sure, I have a top-of-the-line DeWalt sliding, compound miter saw that cuts perfect angles every time and is *almost* idiot-proof, but what if the power goes out in the middle of a project? I might need that old miter box.

And that wooden tennis racket with the wooden brace to keep it from warping? It's true that I haven't set foot on a tennis court in thirty years, but I might take it up in retirement. Well, probably not, but still, it's not easy to get rid of an old classic.

There is some clutter I could stand to get rid of, and it's true—there's a lot of junk in my garage and barn. The problem is, I don't get around to cleaning it up because . . . well . . . I don't care.

The little woman, on the other hand, likes to downsize, and when the mood strikes, she throws good stuff—my stuff—away. She has more shoes than Payless or Imelda Marcos. There are many she's never worn and never will, but they continue to fill the shelves and boxes in her closet. My collection of antique Moxie bottles, on the other hand, disappeared last spring. Winnie's defense was, "They were so old, I couldn't even take them back to the store for the nickel deposit refund." *Ugh!*

And then, there was the mysterious disappearance of my favorite magazine collection. I had dozens of issues of a periodical that contained fascinating articles about Hugh Hefner's mansion and cars, as well as pictorials featuring some of the finest students at America's major universities—our future leaders—all discarded as yesterday's news.

I wouldn't mind losing my good stuff so much if I could at least sell it for a few bucks. Winnie hates to have a yard sale. We tried it once and it didn't work out so well. After a week of selecting, cleaning, fixing, and pricing our old stuff (my old stuff) for sale, we were ready for the advertised 8:30 a.m. start of our sell-off. By 7:30, we'd already had three eager shoppers knocking on our door, asking when the sale started.

"Eight-thirty, just like it says in the *Smalltown News* and on all of our signs," the little woman replied. She's a little grumpy before her first coffee.

The sale started at 8:31 a.m. There were already ten or more carloads of eager shoppers waiting to buy (steal) our stuff. We were anxious to clean house, so everything was priced to sell.

Jake and Maggie's old bikes were marked at $25 each, and Winnie let them go for $15, for the pair. My old set of golf clubs became the property of the first person to wave a $10 bill at the little woman.

Winnie was feeling good about seeing hundreds of pounds of "junk" leave our driveway. To her way of thinking, the yard sale was going well . . . until Mrs. Beazley, from down the street, made an offer on an afghan blanket.

My wife gets bored each winter and crochets while sitting in front of the boob tube, watching reruns of *Monk* and *Murder, She Wrote*. She's produced at least one new afghan for each of the past twenty winters. As a result, we have more blankets than beds and couches so, reluctantly, she decided to sell some of her handiwork at the yard sale. (It's probably meaningful to note here that each of these lovely creations represents at least a hundred hours of labor and several skeins of yarn.)

Mrs. Beazley didn't end up taking home one of these fine afghans, but did leave our dooryard with a loud and concise suggestion for what she could do with her $5 bill.

Will This Winter Ever End?

I DON'T HATE WINTER. In fact, I have to admit, I feel a sort of warped sense of excitement in anticipation of a big blizzard— in December and January. But this winter, it seems as though it just won't stop snowing! It snows twice a week—Monday through Wednesday, and Friday to Sunday. Thursdays have been pleasant.

It seems there is no end to the shoveling this year. And there has been a lot of heavy snow, especially now that it's March and we get a foot of snow followed by a few inches of rain with each storm. Each shovelful weighs ten pounds, or more. It can break a person's back, all that lifting. How can I relax and enjoy the March Madness basketball tournament knowing that the little woman is out there in the cold, driving rain, lifting all that snow over a five-foot snowbank? It's really taking the fun out of it for me. I had to wait until after half-time for her to come in and make my pizza!

I can't remember a winter in Smalltown with this much snow. My roof had to be shoveled three times in the past four weeks! I missed two Celtics games, a golf tournament, and three episodes of *Everybody Loves Raymond* because the little woman is afraid of heights and makes me hold the ladder for her while she shovels the roof. I should just hire the neighbor kid to hold the ladder for her.

Thoughts of an Average Joe

All that snow coming off the roof is banking up against the house. The clapboards will likely need paint in the spring. That doesn't seem to bother Winnie. She doesn't understand how annoying it is to hear all her scraping and wire-brushing while I'm trying to enjoy the Masters tournament on TV.

I'm tired of jackets, boots, gloves, and hats. The snowbanks and my white pickup truck are gray with dirt and sand; there are huge speed-bump frost heaves and potholes the size of a Toyota Prius; and now that the snow is melting and refreezing, I've fallen on my keister four times in the past week. It hurts to sit on the couch—a big problem for me. *I'm sick of winter!*

It'll be great once the snow melts away in May or June. The grass will start to grow; the lawn will need de-thatching and raking to rid it of the leaves and dead branches that have come down since last fall. Flowers will need to be planted in the ground, the vegetable garden will need composting, and seeds will need to be planted. In June and July, the lawn will need to be mowed twice a week. The gardens will need fertilizing and weeding. *And I'm expected to help out with all that.* Oh, and the little woman wants me to replace the rotten boards on the deck because she keeps falling through! She hasn't gained any weight, either; she made that very clear when I asked her. The deck will take up two of the ten weekends of my summer!

The lawn on each side of my driveway will need to be graded and reseeded where my buddy, Barney, landscaped for me while plowing this winter. He doesn't charge me extra for the sod removal.

The asphalt driveway needs to be sealed this summer. That has to be done on the sunniest (and, therefore, hottest) Saturday and Sunday of the summer—two days I'd rather spend with my friend, Roy, on his party boat, fishing and enjoying an occasional wobbly pop. It'll ruin another weekend, a pair of Nikes, and my most comfortable pair of jeans.

Come to think of it, the snow is quite beautiful. It should last longer . . . Maybe I'll move closer to the Arctic Circle.

Political Season

THE POLITICAL CAMPAIGN SEASON in this country is too long. Do we really need two years and hundreds of millions of dollars to decide who should lead our nation?

I, like most Americans, have decided whom I will vote for even before the campaign begins: it's the person running against the candidate I hate. So spare me the baloney, and send me a check for my share of the millions spent trying to convince me. It's a waste of money; and furthermore, all those repetitious, mean-spirited ads interrupt the ball games and reruns of *Everybody Loves Raymond* I'm trying to enjoy.

There are too many campaign signs, too! It really annoys me to see six identical signs along a thirty-yard stretch of roadway. I'll be damned if I'm going to give my vote to any candidate who thinks I'm so stupid that I have to read his or her message six times in six seconds in order to get it.

Did you ever think of what happens to all those signs after the elections? I'm guessing most of them are clogging up our landfills. Some of us pay a dollar a bag to use the landfill. Why not charge candidates a buck a sign? I think it might improve their respect for my intelligence.

One way we could shorten the season is to have a six-week campaign, in which candidates compete for the office to which they aspire through some *Survivor*-like contest that measures grit, common sense, and integrity. For instance,

Survivor Smalltown might pit the final remaining member of the Holstein Tribe against the winner of the Jersey Tribe primary in an immunity challenge which involves producing the most farm income at a time when raw milk is garnering only $12 per 100 pounds, and the cost of fuel to run feed-harvesting equipment is hovering around $4 per gallon. The selectman election would likely go to the candidate wise enough to sell his or her herd (albeit, reluctantly) for beef and his or her pastures for house lots.

I'm sure there are a few politicians out there who truly want to serve their constituents for the right reasons, but there are plenty of nut-jobs, too. I'm not saying we should totally scrap the electoral system upon which this great nation was founded; I just think it needs some serious tweaking.

Deer season is way too short and the political season is way too long. Maybe we should lengthen the season for deer, shorten the season for politicians, and increase the bag limit for both.

Give the Ump a Break

MY BROTHER K.C. is a fair amount younger than I am, so consequently, his kids are a lot younger than Jake and Maggie. His boy Eli plays Little League baseball, and K.C. volunteers to be an umpire for the league.

I'm not sure why anyone would sign up for that job. It's a thankless position, and besides, who needs umps on the field when there are a dozen or so keen-sighted, well-informed, loudmouthed parents in the bleachers who are more than happy to render an opinion on each pitch or play.

There's something about watching her little boy play that seems to turn even the most pleasant woman into an over-protective, raving maniac. Betsy Peters is a nurse over at the Smalltown Medical Clinic. When I go to see Dr. Braley about my little problem (the nature of which is none of your business, by the way), you could sweeten your tea with the kind words that drip off her tongue. But sit her backside on one of those pine planks, and she becomes a fiercely opinionated Momzilla.

"He was safe!" Betsy yelled when her little darling popped out to the pitcher as Timmy ran from home plate to *third* base. "That was a hit, ump. You're gonna cost my Timmy a scholarship with calls like that."

I'm sorry, Betsy, but first of all, this is Little League. More importantly, Timmy's name and any form of the word *scholar* shouldn't be used in the same sentence. It's like Rosie O'Donnell and Sarah Palin (or any other intelligent, attractive woman). They don't belong together.

K.C. was calling balls and strikes behind home plate for an all-star game last week and getting way too much static from Lynette Goyet, from nearby St. Jamesboro.

"That weren't no strike, ump. Get yer eyes checked!" she yelled in her high-pitched, fingernails-on-the-chalkboard voice.

K.C. showed considerable restraint, especially for a guy with a reputation for having a short fuse. He's grown up a lot since he broke Junior Wilson's nose over a receding-hairline comment.

Lynette had "helped" K.C. call the game for five innings, and I know my little brother well enough to realize his patience was wearing as thin as late-April ice on Shadow Lake. I cringed when Lynette's chubby kid, Georgie, stepped up to the plate.

Georgie swung wildly at the first two pitches, missing each by a foot or so, and then took a partial swing at the third offering. K.C. said he went around and was out on strike three.

Lynette went ballistic. She was on the field and in my brother's face before little Georgie could waddle back to the dugout.

"He didn't swing," she screamed. "You're an idiot!"

"And you're ugly," K.C. retorted, drawing cheers from most of the crowd.

"What did you say?" Lynette asked.

"You heard me."

"Well, I demand that you ask the third-base ump . . ."

K.C. walked down the third-base line to confer with Ike Masure and then returned to home plate.

"Ike said that I made an accurate call . . . and by the way, he said Georgie was out, too."

Do It Yourself

I'M A FRUGAL GUY. Winnie says I'm a cheapskate. I don't like to waste money. I frequently do, but I don't like to—especially when it comes to home repairs.

My buddy Barney has a small-engine repair business. There's a sign near his service counter which explains his labor rates. It reads something like this:

LABOR: $30/HR

IF YOU WANT TO HELP: $40/HR

IF YOU'VE ALREADY TRIED TO FIX PROBLEM: $50/HR

I've paid the $50-per-hour rate many times. Last summer, the little woman's riding lawn mower needed a simple belt replacement. There was no way I was paying Barney $30 per hour to do an easy repair like that. So I drove the old Eagle Star up onto some car ramps and crawled under her. There were pulleys and gears and belts in every direction. I had an owner's manual (and I took a year of Spanish back in high school), so it took me only two hours to figure out how to remove the main drive pulley to get to the left serpentine pulley so I could replace the belt.

The repair was complicated by the fact that my metric socket set was in my camper, which was at Dick's RV Repair, to replace a fitting on the water heater I'd broken by over-tightening a nut.

Anyway, two hours later, the serpentine belt was replaced, and even though in the meantime I'd missed the final game of the World Series, I was pleased with myself. I fired up the old tractor, drove onto my front lawn, and engaged the mower deck. And didn't the Eagle Star cut a pretty, smooth swatch—about ten yards long—before I heard the ominous sound of clanging pulleys and flopping belts! Not a problem. Three days and $150 later, Barney had her fixed up good as new.

Winnie decided we needed one of those fancy one-lever faucets, with the spray hose and all, to replace the one that came with our house, thirty years ago. She picked up a fixture she liked down at Smalltown Hardware and called up Jacky Spencer to see what he'd charge to install it. No way was I going to give that knucklehead plumber $80 to come over and loosen a few fittings to install a simple faucet. Jacky was the dumbest guy in my class. He made it through eighth grade only because he was sixteen years old and had been at Small-town Elementary longer than any of the teachers there. So, I took a day off from work and commenced to putting in the little woman's faucet.

There I am, wedged under the kitchen sink, my head and shoulders between half-empty containers of Comet Cleanser and Kibbles 'n Bits, channel-lock pliers (the tool guaranteed to strip the corners off any nut) and vise grips (designed to pinch that soft pad between the pinky finger and wrist and leave a painful bruise) at the ready. I twisted and grunted and cursed until I realized I was turning the nut in the wrong direction because I was . . . well . . . upside down and backwards. So I reversed directions with my wrenches. Finally, the nut let go all of sudden, sending me sideways under the cabinet and reminding me, in the midst of the maneuver, that I'd forgotten one very important step.

By now, I was covered with about two gallons of water and had knocked over a bottle of ammonia, the cap of which Winnie hadn't secured very well. So, there I was, soaked in lukewarm water and smelling like I'd wet myself, when the little woman walked into the room.

"So, how's it going, Einstein?" she innocently inquired.

"Oh, it's going really well," I yelled, ammonia-scented water dripping from my eyebrows. "You can call your friend Jacky now; tell him I've done the hard stuff, and he can take over from here."

I Like a Good Steak

I LIKE MEAT. I think human beings are intended to eat beef, pork, chicken, fish, venison, moose, etc. God gave us sharp teeth for that very reason. We even have teeth called "canine incisors"—teeth like dogs, wolves, coyotes, and other meat-eating species. Our creator wants us to eat meat.

I have friends who are vegetarians. I can understand people who don't like the flavor or texture of meat; I don't eat spinach for the same reason. It tastes funny, and it makes my teeth feel weird. What I don't understand are people who don't eat animal flesh because they love all critters. They say, "I won't eat anything with a face." They can't stand the idea of an animal having to die to feed another. "It's so cruel."

I can't think of one vegetarian who doesn't own a cat or dog. Think about it—what do they feed their pets? When I go to Small-Mart to buy food for the little woman's cat, I see Ocean Fish, Turkey Feast, and Chicken and Beef Delight, but never Carrots and Turnip Entree. That's because cats, like me, love meat. They eat grass and other plants only when they want to make themselves vomit. Outdoor cats never bring home a daisy or an apple to please their human friend. They lug home something with a face—a mouse or a chickadee. They've seen our teeth, and they know we eat meat.

The dogs that vegetarians love so much like meat, too. I guess they make some dog foods out of soybeans and other

252

vegetables, but dogs prefer meat. Most of them will eat anything, even their frozen poop, but they prefer meat. If you
doubt that, drop a T-bone steak and a rutabaga in front of
Fido and see which disappears first. It's the poor little crit-
ter with the face that had to die to make your precious Fido
happy.

It must be inconvenient to be a vegetarian. Most restaurants
offer no more than one plant-based entrée. That's because
most people want to eat meat as the main course, because it's
nature's way. And what about holiday traditions? Who invites
friends and family over for a Thanksgiving cabbage with
stuffing and all the fixings? And Tofurky? Don't even get me
started, my vegetarian friends. Don't serve me fake turkey, and
I won't try to sneak a slice of mincemeat pie into your belly.

Some folks won't even consume dairy products or eggs. I'm
not likely to order a Grande Mocha Latte with soy milk, and I
like a good omelet (though I do have to wonder if, long ago,
two guys were standing in the barnyard when one turned to
his buddy and said, "Let's eat the next thing that comes out of
that hen's rear end").

Most of you have probably seen a T-shirt that reads VEG-
ETARIAN—AN OLD INDIAN WORD MEANING LOUSY HUNTER. I take
exception to that. I don't shoot many deer, and I certainly
couldn't feed my family with the venison I've harvested over
the years. But that's because I'm very selective. I'm a trophy
hunter. That's my story and I'm sticking to it.

Happy Snowman-Burning Day

I LIKE SOME HOLIDAYS. I like to pig out on Thanksgiving Day, and Christmas has always been fun. (Too bad the season lasts so long, because I get tired of Christmas carols by early December.) I also like Independence Day. Up here in the North Country, it's really the beginning of summer; Labor Day is the end. All of these holidays are good for a paid day off. What's not to like about that?

Recently, I stumbled upon a list of holidays I'd never heard of. It made me realize that many holidays are the invention of greeting card companies and newspaper advertising departments, and others are the brainchildren of people with too little to do. I swear to you, I didn't make up any of these days.

Did you know that January 1 is more than New Year's Day? It is also Bad Hangover Day. It's true that lots of people start off the year suffering from dehydration, fatigue, headache, diarrhea, nausea, vomiting, flatulence, anxiety, irritability, and sensitivity to light, but that hardly seems like something to celebrate.

January 27 is Thomas Crapper Day, a day devoted to the memory of the man who allegedly invented the flush toilet in the 1880s. I wonder . . . How does one celebrate this holiday? Do you read a book while sitting on porcelain? Bob for apples? Send the goldfish (the one you inherited after the kids moved out) on an adventure?

Be sure to mark April 23 on your calendar. That's National Nose-Picking Day. And, why not? Rhinotillexis is an essentially universal activity. Studies indicate that humans clean the dried mucous from our nasal passages an average of four times a day. Some folks celebrate National Nose-Picking Day by counting the number of people they observe practicing rhinotillexis while enjoying a meal in their favorite restaurant. Sounds appetizing.

June 2 has been designated National Bubba Day. This is a day to throw a party for anyone nicknamed Bubba. In Smalltown, that affects only two people that I know of, but I suspect it is nearly impossible to get an oil change in Jackson, Mississippi, on the second day of June.

On June 13 each year some people observe the World Naked Bike Ride by participating in a clothing-optional bicycle ride, "to protest oil dependency and celebrate the power and individuality of our bodies." I'm sorry, but few people look good naked, even standing still, to say nothing of how they look while pedaling a bike. The visual just isn't pretty—too many moving parts. I hope they wear a helmet at least; heaven forbid that someone observing such a holiday would suffer brain damage.

Be Late for Something Day is officially September 5—something my sister celebrates every day.

September 6 is Fight Procrastination Day. It also happens to be my birthday (really), so I guess I'll celebrate it later.

Clean Out Your Refrigerator Day is November 14. Really? Only once a year?

December 3 is Make Up Your Mind Day. I'm not sure if I'll celebrate it or not. I might, I might not; I can't decide.

What is Put On Your Own Shoes Day? I couldn't find much information about this one, so I'm not sure if it is intended to encourage young children to dress themselves, or for the rest of us to celebrate feeling comfortable "walking your own path in life," or if December 3 is a day my buddy Munzie should wear penny loafers instead of dressing up in his sister's stiletto heels.

There are some holidays we should all observe: Memorial Day, Labor Day, and Veterans Day come to mind. But I'm not likely to miss work for Read in the Bathtub Day, Wave *All* Your Fingers at Your Neighbor Day, or Dump Your Significant Jerk Day. I will probably, however, stay home on Working Naked Day.

The World Is Full of Stupid Drivers

Is IT JUST ME, or are there more stupid drivers on the road these days? I don't drive all that much. It's about five miles from my home to my workplace, so you'd think I could negotiate those ten miles a day without wanting to take a life. The problem, I've decided, is that while one has to pass a road test to drive, a person can obtain a license to operate a dangerous vehicle without any measurement of intelligence, common sense, or human courtesy. Does that scare anyone else?

There's an intersection on my short commute home that requires me to wait at a traffic light for several minutes. That's several dangerous minutes for me to sit and stew in anticipation of what nearly always happens when it's my turn to go. For this particular intersection on a state highway, some ingenious engineer, apparently one with a sadistic sense of humor, decided that the flow of traffic from the south, east, and west should be controlled by a light, *but let's allow the nice folks coming from the north to decide for themselves if they should recognize the yield sign governing their traffic flow.* I can tell you, without hesitation, that most of them, especially those in a hurry to get their Hummers back downcountry, don't yield.

To make things worse, they tend to respond to my light-flashing, horn-honking, tailgating rage with a hand gesture. You'd think they could at least apologize for their ignorance by waving with their entire hand . . . they're number-one with me too! Makes me wish I still owned that rusty old F-350 with a heavy-duty bumper handcrafted from two-by-ten rough-cut hemlock.

The other folks that make my blood percolate a bit are the young drivers who are so important that they can't get out of their own driveway without restoring contact with the other important people of the wireless world.

So there I sit, at a stop sign waiting my turn, when around the corner, turning left in front of me, is a multitasking, twenty-year-old mother. I can tell she's a mom because of the CAUTION—BABY ON BOARD sign in her side window. She negotiates the corner practically on two wheels and just misses my front bumper. She offers no hand gestures, though, leaving me to wonder why. Is it because of the baby on board, or is it that she has a phone in her left hand and a latté and the steering wheel in her right hand?

Is it just me . . . ?

I'd Vote for an Honest Politician

HOW REFRESHING WOULD IT BE to have an Average Joe, say Joe Schmo, throw his hat into the political ring—any political ring—and tell it like it really is. I'd vote for a guy (or gal) who told us how he really feels, instead of what he thinks we want to hear. Imagine the following at a press conference:

"Mr. Schmo, do you really think you can win this election?"

"That's a stupid question . . . Next."

"If elected, do you think you can make a difference for the people of this state?"

"I don't know. I'm running because I just lost my job, and I figure this one pays well, requires little effort, and comes with good benefits and great perks. I hear I'd have a staff, two interns, and a driver . . . *Sweet!*"

"Joe . . ."

"I don't know you. Call me Mr. Schmo."

"Sorry, umm, Mr. Schmo. If elected, what will you do about this country's huge budget deficit?"

"Duh! I think we might need to spend less than we bring in. That'll mean no more free rides. Every able-bodied citizen will have to get a job and pull his or her own weight. No more handouts for the lazy buggers who won't work."

"But, Mr. Schmo, some people don't want to work."

"It sucks to be them. They can get a job, or move to some other country stupid enough to take care of them."

"Candidate Schmo, are there leaders who have been an inspiration to you?"

"Yes, ma'am. I admire former presidents Kennedy and Clinton, and Senator Gary Hart."

"Because they were strong leaders with common values and personal charisma?"

"No, ma'am—'cause they all had hot girlfriends while in office. Next question."

"So, if I understand you correctly, Mr. Schmo, you want to be elected for the money, the driver, and the women."

"I'm glad someone is paying attention. Thank you. Next . . . You sir, in the pink shirt."

"What is your position on same-sex marriage?"

"It's fine with me. My wife and I have been having the same sex for over thirty years. Besides, I believe you fellas should have the same right to be as miserable as the rest of us straight dudes."

"Candidate Schmo, a lot of Americans are concerned about immigration. Do you feel we should tighten security at our borders?"

"Heck, no! We need to let a few more of those Canadians through. How else are we gonna get good hockey players?"

"If I may follow up, I think there is more concern about the Mexican border. Do you have a plan for controlling immigration there?"

"Well, in fact, I do. I propose an exchange program where for each Mexican we allow into our country, we get to send one of our folks there, and I get to choose."

"Could you elaborate for us, Mr. Schmo?"

"I'd be happy to. Let me give you an example. Let's say Juan, Maria, and Pedro want to cross the border into the United States. Then, I could, in exchange, send Rosie, O.J., and Hillary."

I'd vote for Joe Schmo, wouldn't you?

About the Author

BRIAN DANIELS IS AN AVID OUTDOORSMAN, a newspaper columnist, novelist, musician, and songwriter. Many of his songs, including four title tracks, have been recorded by eight different artists. His first novel, *Luke's Dream*, was released in January 2011. He has written a humorous column for several years, "Thoughts of an Average Joe by Joe Wright," which is featured in newspapers throughout northern New England. His blog, "Thoughts of an Average Joe," can be seen at avgjoewright.blogspot.com. Brian was born and raised in Vermont's "Northeast Kingdom." His childhood hometown, Lyndonville, serves as inspiration for Average Joe's Smalltown. Since 1984, he has practiced optometry in Brunswick, Maine, where he lives with his wife, Laurene.